HIW

D1438693

it at:
ov.uk
4 800 8006
rd & PIN ready

ONE GIRL AND HER DOGS

ONE GIRL AND HER DOGS

Life, Love and Lambing in the Middle of Nowhere

Emma Gray

with Barbara Fox

WINDSOR
PARAGON

First published 2012
by Sphere
This Large Print edition published 2012
by AudioGO Ltd
by arrangement with
Little, Brown Book Group

Hardcover   ISBN: 978 1 4713 0715 7
Softcover   ISBN: 978 1 4713 0716 4

Copyright © Emma Gray 2012
Poem copyright © Archie Tait 2012

The moral right of the author has been asserted

All rights reserved.

British Library Cataloguing in Publication Data available

NORFOLK LIBRARY AND
INFORMATION SERVICE

SUPPLIER	AudioGO
INVOICE No.	
ORDER DATE	4.2.13
COPY No.	GRA

Printed and bound in Great Britain by
MPG Books Group Limited

To Mum and Dad, Caroline and Elizabeth

Thanks to my parents Richard and Helen and all my grandparents for love, support and inspiration, to my sisters Caroline and Elizabeth for being there to share things with and to Dan for being here now. And to all the friends and fellow farmers who have helped me over the years. Thanks to Hannah Boursnell and her team at Little, Brown Book Group for giving me the chance to tell my tale, to Barbara Fox, who worked with me on this book, to Sian Wilson who designed the cover, and to Sarah Castleton who made helpful improvements to the text.

Chapter One

I hate getting up in the mornings. If I could, I would snuggle in bed all day long, but that is a luxury I cannot afford—so I am forced to take decisive action. Step one: I have equipped myself with the world's noisiest alarm clock. This thing can probably wake the dead and I have set it to unleash its unholy racket at six o'clock on the dot. Rather than keep it by the bedside, though—and this is step two—I place it on the opposite side of the room, out of arms' reach, so that I can't simply silence it with a swat and sink back into my lovely warm duvet. Instead, when I can stand the din no longer—when my ears are on the point of bleeding—I groan, heave myself up from my nest and make a dash across a freezing cold room to switch it off. Mission accomplished. It is a rude awakening . . . but that seems to be the story of my life at the moment.

I still can't quite believe that I am living back at home with Mum and Dad, at the age of twenty-three, six years after I moved out. I have been back for a few weeks now but it still takes me by surprise to wake up and realise I'm in my childhood bedroom in my parents' farmhouse and that my fiancé, Steven, is not here with me.

My room has not changed much since I was last here. The same books line the shelves and my rosettes are still pinned to the walls. I half expect to see my teenage self sitting on a beanbag, nose in a dog-training manual. The walls themselves have had a lick of paint since then, but I can see a ghost of the garish orange I opted for in a moment of ill-judged teenage rebellion. I have to smile—it was truly frightful—but my smile quickly fades as the present reality sinks in. The room may be the same, but the girl in it is not.

I am back here because I said goodbye to the man I have been with for the past four years, the man I was going to marry. I just packed up my bags and left. The first thing everyone wants to know is: why? 'I don't know,' I tell them, feebly. 'I just felt that something was missing.' And that's about the long and short of it. I just couldn't ignore the cloud that pursued me like an ominous forewarning. Nothing was particularly *wrong* between Steven and me; I wasn't exactly unhappy; I just knew in my heart that it wasn't the life I was supposed to be living, and that nothing would work out unless I tried to find out what was missing. I feel so bad about it all. I know everyone thinks it was a stupid, rash, selfish thing to do—and they're probably right—but I know deep down that I *am* doing the right thing.

It's October, and the view from the window—overcast sky, grey drizzle falling—is not exactly cheering, but the thought of the dogs waiting to be let out lifts up my spirits and spurs me to drag on some clothes and head downstairs.

Bess is still asleep in the kitchen. Once upon a time she would greet me with mad barks of joy but now she merely looks up, flaps her tail once and goes back to sleep. She is another one I hurt by leaving—but that was a long time ago. She was my first dog, my best friend, but when I wasn't there any more she transferred her doting affections to Mum, and I think of her as Mum's dog now. Things between us will never be the same again, but they are improving. When I first came home she couldn't bear to be in

2

the same room as me. Now she will tolerate my presence as long as I don't make a fuss. At work, it is a different story: out in the fields we still have the same connection we always did.

My first *real* hello is waiting for me outside: Fly, Roy and Alfie.

Fly is as good as her name. She jumps with joy the moment she sees me—she can reach my full height and can even clear the six-foot run her kennel is in, though she would never do so unless I called for her. Roy is more reserved and only wants a pat before heading off to make sure he has marked everything in sight. Alfie is eager for attention, doing his full body wag, banging repeatedly against my legs in an effort to steal the limelight.

I let them run around for a bit but at my command they all leap into my battered Ford pickup. It is not the most glamorous set of wheels, but it is reliable and the back has been separated into compartments to minimise opportunities for doggy confrontations—a godsend now that we spend up to three hours a day on the road.

I am a shepherdess, looking after nine hundred sheep at Fairspring Farm in Northumberland, a good sixty miles away from Mum and Dad's farm, Muirfield, in Hawick in the Scottish Borders. I am determined to keep my job. Fairspring is a fantastic farm. I love it to bits and after four years working there, it almost feels like my own. It has a great range of fields, from gorsy hills we know as 'the banks' to a cluster of smaller hayfields, and a canal that runs straight through it—very picturesque, but a total pain whenever the lambs decide to see if they can swim across.

But the journey is taking its toll. I could really do

without the physical strain of all that driving, not to mention the extra financial cost involved. My diesel bills have rocketed—so much so that I have been forced to dip into my savings. The journey is stretching me to my limits. I am desperate to find somewhere closer to live and I keep my eye out for To Let signs as I trundle along. The dogs are subdued during the long drive, but the second we bump over the cattle grid on the final approach to Fairspring they are on their paws and yipping with excitement. We made it!

*　　　*　　　*

It is Friday and that means the *Hexham Courant* is out. As I have been doing every Friday for weeks now, I turn straight to the property section to scour the rental adverts. A soul-defeating pattern has emerged. I will find a place that sounds just right—something close to Fairspring, affordable on my small salary. When I phone up, I get on swimmingly with the landlord and everything is fine—until I mention that I have three collies, four if you include my old dog Bill (but he will stay at my parents' until I am more settled). From then on in my hopes will begin to deflate, slowly but surely, like a punctured tyre. I explain how farm dogs are extremely well behaved, happy to live outside, are ever so quiet, and out with me all day anyway—but it doesn't seem to make any difference. It is like a three-letter curse. Nobody wants a d-o-g—or even worse, d-o-g-s.

My dogs are my life, though, and I'm not going anywhere without them. They are the tools of my trade and my loyal friends, constant companions

4

through thick and thin. We are a team. Sometimes I think they understand me better than any human being can; they even seem to be in touch with my moods, knowing instinctively when I am sad and in need of an affectionate nuzzle, or when their light-hearted japes are just what is required to distract me from my troubles.

Today's paper lists an advert for a place about half an hour's drive from Fairspring. Marlene Cottage. It is a bit farther out than is ideal, but still, I am excited because I know the owners and I guess that might stand me in better stead than usual. They invite me over to take a look round. It is a small house on two levels: a kitchen, a living room and a bathroom downstairs, and a bedroom upstairs in the attic space. There is no central heating but in a place this cosy a coal fire works a charm. The warmth rushes up to hug me the moment I step over the threshold—it's like my beloved duvet, in house form. I'm in love.

I gather the wherewithal to mention the d-o-g-s. It takes a little bit of chat and some negotiation but eventually we reach an agreement—they will let me put up my kennels in the back garden on the condition that I keep the collies quiet. Village life is unforgiving and it is in everyone's best interests to avoid rubbing the neighbours up the wrong way. We shake hands on it, there and then. I'm back in the Ford and driving away before it sinks in. I can move out of my parents' house and get back to Northumberland; and I can finally do something about forging the future I gave up so much for. My life will certainly be different at Marlene Cottage. I'll be living on my own, away from a farm for the first time, right in the heart of a small village . . . But there is a pub a short walk away, and of course I have my dogs to keep me company and the villagers will take me under their wing, there's bound to be heaps going on, plenty of new friends. If this is the new start I have been looking for, I tell myself, then I think I'm going to like it.

* * *

I gather the last of the lambs. They have been in the shed for four weeks, deeply bedded on good straw and with carefully balanced rations of high quality feed to help them fatten. Today they are going to another farm to fatten further before they are sold for slaughter.

Most of the lambs left Fairspring over the last few weeks of the summer when they were four or five months old, straight off the grass with no extra feeding whatsoever, but the quality of the grass is poorer now that it's October, and those lambs which didn't fatten need to be cosseted so that they stay warm and channel all their resources into putting on weight. Their problems usually date back to lambing time. Perhaps they had an older mother than the rest, who did not milk as well as the younger ewes; or maybe they were one of triplets and lost the battle at feeding time. Either way they start out on the back foot.

Among this lot are a few of the pet lambs. Pet lambs are infinitely different from the others. They might look the same to the untrained eye, but I can pick them out for the air of superiority they wear like a royal robe. They lack the normal instincts of a sheep. This has some distinct disadvantages, one of which is that they have no fear. Rather than keep with the pack they will often wander off wherever they please, carelessly leading a trail of followers over the hills and far away.

As I clip the lambs' tails and attach ear tags to identify them as the property of Fairspring, I hear the washer-board swoosh of wheels rumbling over the two broken cattle grids on the mile-long track leading up to the farm—this sound is always my first alert to my visitors' arrivals. The wagon is on its way.

The wagon is bright red and the words PATRICK BROS. are emblazoned in gold across the front. It does a deft spin in the yard and backs up to the sheep pens. I wave it in, 'Keep coming, keep coming. Whoa!'

Hylton is the driver and co-owner of a fleet of wagons as well as running a farm of his own. We have a well-oiled routine now, he and I, having repeated this same job at least once a week almost every week since the late summer. The drill commences without much ceremony. Down drops the wagon's tailgate whereupon we shush the sheep up the ramps and on to the top deck. The door swings shut and that's it. They are as good as gone.

'Bet you're pleased to see the back of that lot, eh?' says Hylton with a grin.

'Yeah, they're a lot of work.'

He asks me if I have found anywhere to live yet and I tell him about the cottage.

'Ah, I was thinking of you the other day. There's a little farm just a few mile from me that's come up to let.' He looks at me and pauses, sensing my interest.

'Go on.'

'Aye, it's through the National Trust. They call it Fallowlees. You're probably not bothered now, but you can always give them a ring and get the particulars. Mind, it's a rough sort of spot, very remote, no mains

7

electric, stuck in the trees.'

'Sounds like it'll suit me down to the ground,' I say, with a giggle, half joking. But the moment he's gone I go and look up the number for the National Trust.

*   *   *

I moved in to Marlene Cottage two weeks ago. It's a Saturday night, the pub is just down the road, and what am I doing? I am staying in on my own by the fireside. All those fantasies I had about village life, about being at the heart of the community! It would be funny if it wasn't so tragic. I have been thinking about my friends, going through the names of people I could call, but it only makes me realise how many of them I met through Steven. Even if I did pluck up the courage to call, I am pretty sure none of them would want anything to do with me. They probably wouldn't even answer the phone.

I'm not going to get any sympathy from anyone, that's for sure, least of all Mum and Dad. They are both still in shock—they are very fond of Steven and they cannot believe I could do something like this to him. Sometimes I think that Dad sees Steven as the son he never had. Maybe that is not quite the case, but I know they both hoped that it was just a silly phase, that I would see sense soon enough and go back to him. In my darker moments I wonder whether they are right, that it was a case of 'out of the frying pan and into the fire'—but those moments never last long. I made the right decision, the hardest decision, and I just have to trust that the rest of the world will see it that way too, in time.

Right now, I have my work to keep me going.

Shepherding can be a solitary occupation and there are days when I find I've spoken more to the dogs and the sheep than to my fellow humans (come to think of it, most days are like that) but at least when I'm on the farm with the animals for company, I feel—no, it's stronger than that, I *know*—that I am wanted.

Perhaps this is why I have not been able to stop thinking about Fallowlees since Hylton told me about it.

I have let the dogs inside to stretch out in the warmth. A lot of farmers have strong views about their working dogs and don't allow them in the house, but mine come in and potter about like members of the family. Fly stirs and opens an adoring eye to check on me before closing it again. I have had Fly for almost four years, since she was tiny, the only black and white pup in a litter of blue merles. After everyone had taken their pick of the more unusual blues she was the only one left and I'm just thankful that nobody else took a shine to her. From the word go, the two of us have been a team. I was not an experienced trainer, but she and I worked through it all together, both learning as we went. She is the most loyal dog I will ever own. She will sit and gaze into my eyes. I am her world. She does not have the strength of some sheepdogs, but what she lacks in raw power she more than makes up for in pure effort. If I were to set her an impossible task, she would persevere to her last breath rather than let me down. Whether we are out checking the sheep, gathering lambs for dosing or just sitting together in my car, having lunch and listening to Radio 1, we are inseparable. I doubt I will ever own another dog like her.

Roy is the Casanova of the dog world. Like a cocky young lad strutting about in a bar eyeing the pretty girls before charming them with cheesy chat-up lines, Roy is convinced he is God's gift. And just like those lads at the bar, it never ceases to amaze me how often it works! Surround him with female trial dogs and he is in his element. But he's also my best work dog, a real powerhouse, and has such presence that the sheep know that he's the boss as soon as he comes into contact with them.

He is very intelligent and always seems to know what is required of him. I can trust Roy to do anything, whether it's bringing in the big aggressive tups (male sheep) or gently catching a baby lamb that's become separated from its mother.

Alfie is six months Roy's junior and twice Roy's size but he has deferred to Roy ever since he was a puppy—he still worships him. Alfie is the goon in the team: think of Scooby-Doo with the brains of Homer Simpson. People often can't believe he's a collie because he is as smooth as a piglet and built like a lurcher with long legs and a deep chest. He is a true athlete and can run for miles and miles without tiring. Dog owners call it 'having a good engine'. He is obedient to the last—but sometimes 'obedient' can be another word for 'stupid'. If I ask him to lie down and then get side-tracked, he will stay glued to the very spot until eventually I come looking for him ten minutes later. I could take sheep out the same gate every day for a week and on day seven Alfie would still need to be told what to do. But he is a great work dog and very honest, and no matter what situation he gets into he is always listening for my commands and has full faith that I will not see him wrong.

Each of my dogs is a rich, rounded character to me, and the more I get to know them, the more interesting and inspiring they become. Yet if it were not for my grandpa, I might never have discovered the joys of having my own dog and—who knows?—I might not have gone on to do the job I so adore. When I was growing up my dad could not see any need for me to have a dog of my own. We already had an old farm dog and although she was no great shakes as a sheepdog, she could just about do what was required of her. My desperate pleas for a puppy continued to fall on deaf ears.

Then one day, Grandpa rolled up in his battered old Trooper. A visit from Grandpa was a rare treat; he had his own farm to run in Northumberland and was always busy. My sisters, Caroline and Elizabeth, and I looked forward to his visits like mad.

'I've got a present for the girls,' he announced to Mum as he strode into the farmhouse.

It was a late summer's day, and Dad was still out working. I felt a bubble-rush of excitement fizzing through my chest.

'She's in the back,' he said, tilting his head in the direction of the Trooper. We girls dashed into the yard, Grandpa following right behind. We yanked open the mud-splattered door and peered inside. On the back seat was a small, sodden box on top of a pile of old newspapers. Being the eldest, and a real bossy boots, I decided it was my job to open it. My sisters could hardly contain themselves beside me.

'What is it?'

'I can't see!'

'Nor can I!'

I pulled open the lid to reveal, with a gasp, the smallest Border collie pup I had ever seen—hardly

11

more than a bundle of fluff, she was perfect and beautiful down to her last hair. I loved her at first sight but knew I mustn't let myself get carried away. What was Dad going to say when he found out?

'Well, what are you waiting for?' said Grandpa impatiently. 'Get her out of there.'

I saw Mum give him one of her looks. It was a look that said, 'Uh-oh . . .'

I scooped up the tiny scrap and carried her into the kitchen, ignoring Mum's protests. Mum has always been very house-proud and does not like animals inside, and a sodden pup, too young to be housetrained, was hardly likely to change her mind. Fortunately Grandpa was a bit of a charmer and she quickly gave in.

By the time Dad appeared, my sisters and I were happily playing with our new, freshly washed puppy in front of the Aga while Mum and Grandpa looked on.

'What the . . . What is *that* doing here? I'm telling you now, it's not bloody staying!'

All three of our faces crumpled. Grandpa looked at Dad. Dad looked back at him, furious. Mum looked as if she would rather not get involved.

I think if anyone other than Grandpa had been responsible for this new arrival, my dream would have ended there and then. But Grandpa commanded a lot of respect from people, including his own son. He had been a hard taskmaster in his younger years (Dad vouched for that) and although he had mellowed with age, he still tended to get his own way.

Perhaps Grandpa thought that having a dog of your own was a rite of passage all farm children deserved. He himself was a great dog man and had a knack for bringing out the best in them. Although he never trialled, he was well known in the area for having good, capable work dogs.

Between Grandad's authority, Mum's loaded silence, and our three smitten faces, Dad clearly didn't have much choice in the matter.

'Well, if you're going to keep it . . .' He hesitated. I held my breath.

'I say *if*, mind you—*if* you're going to keep it, then it's to be your responsibility and yours alone. Don't expect me to go cleaning up after the damn thing. And it lives *out-side*. No argument.'

The three of us shrieked with delight.

He wasn't exactly over the moon about the whole thing, and it would be a long time before he would admit that having a good dog around *did* bring some benefits, but Bess—as we named her—became a member of the Gray household. And what a member she was!

Although she came from an immaculate line, Bess was the runt of the litter. She was only six weeks old when she came to us (eight to ten weeks is the usual age for pups to leave their mothers), so it was a massive upheaval for her.

Seeing how weedy and rather pot-bellied she looked, Mum decided to worm her that night and allowed her to stay in a cardboard box in the utility room, 'just one night'. I remember how little sleep I got. I was far too excited. A puppy, a real puppy! I lay in bed imagining all the agility and obedience trophies we would win. Most of all, somehow I knew I had just gained a best friend. I might have to share her with my sisters, but I would put up with that if it meant she could stay.

I shot downstairs at the crack of dawn. It felt a bit

like Christmas morning. I flung open the door to the utility room and stopped dead. The smell was appalling. All over the floor were massive piles of faeces covered with worms.

'Mum! Dad! Something's wrong with Bess,' I wailed.

The commotion brought the whole family out of bed. Caroline and Elizabeth were as repulsed by the scene as I was, but Mum seemed to take it in her stride. She explained that these were dog worms and that they were common in young puppies. All it meant was that the medicine had worked and Bess would be fine. I could have cried with relief. Then Mum reminded us that Bess was our puppy and it was our job to clean up the mess. Caroline and Elizabeth shrank away at the prospect, and I wasn't too happy about doing it all on my own if Bess did indeed belong to all three of us. However, I had spotted a golden opportunity for some bargaining. I suggested to my sisters that if I took charge of this unpleasant task, then Bess would become *my* dog. I would allow them to play with her whenever they wanted, but I would be responsible for feeding her, walking her and training her.

They were only too happy to agree to my terms.

Such deviousness in one so young! Such cunning! But in my head it was only fair. *I* was the oldest, *I* had been looking forward to having my own dog far longer than they had, and if all it took was a pair of Marigolds and bit of cleaning to call her mine—then so be it; it was a small price to pay.

Bess turned out to be a little minx. She was into everything. Even though she lived outside—neither Dad nor Mum would relent there—she managed to sneak in at the slightest opportunity and zone in on whatever she should not be messing with. She was attracted to the weirdest household items: she could scissor a zip from an expensive jacket in next to no time, and as for brooms and dishcloths, well, they didn't stand a chance.

Bess and I spent hours in each other's company. I would get up early to take her out in the morning and rush home after school so that I could play with her. I taught her to sit, lie down, play dead, give a paw and hide her face with her paws. I had great hopes of turning her into a superb agility dog—and although she was too young to train properly, she was a quick learner. I taught her to wriggle her way through the concrete pipes the water board had left lying around, and to jump over little hurdles I made with some traffic cones I had acquired from the A7. By the time she was six months old we were trying our hand at sheep gathering, though I was as ignorant about this as she was. I would take her out on a ridiculously long lead—all the books were agreed that this was the best way to keep control of a young dog—and as a result I would be dragged all over the place. It was a wonder my arm remained attached to my shoulder. When it came to enthusiasm, we had it in buckets and there was no challenge we would not put our minds to cracking.

I suppose you could say I became obsessed with my dog in the way that other young girls might become obsessed with horses. When I wasn't with Bess I spent hours poring over training manuals and Border collie books. Actual people didn't get much of a look-in. She was just as devoted to me as I was to her. A collie's love is all-consuming, as near to unconditional as I have ever experienced. I was proud of the fact that Bess would ditch anyone else

15

if she had a chance of being by my side, that I was the only person who could get her to chase sheep and obey commands. She even went so far as to give Dad the odd nip when he was trying to feed the sheep, but was clever enough to do this when he had his hands full and couldn't chase after her. Oh, Bess was my pride and joy!

*   *   *

What happened next was a nightmare. It was a Sunday evening in the run-up to lambing. I was busy finishing some homework that was due in the next day, while Mum and Dad were down in the shed giving the pregnant ewes their night-time feed of silage. Unbeknown to us all, Bess had sneaked along to help them, never liking to miss out on the action.

Dad was driving the telehandler, which we often used for feeding. They are useful machines but with notoriously poor operator visibility. Suddenly, a bloodcurdling noise ripped the night apart. Mum dropped everything and rushed to find Dad. The noise was so human, she said later; it was like someone was being tortured. And it just went on and on. By the time she reached Dad he was crouching over something on the ground. The thing was screaming, screaming.

It was Bess.

'I just didn't see her,' said Dad, clearly upset. He gently examined her, while Mum stood helplessly beside him.

'She's badly damaged, Helen. Her back end is crushed. I'm sorry, but you're going to have to take her to be put down.'

16

He carefully lifted the wrecked creature into the back of the car, telling Mum he would ring the vet so that the surgery would be prepared for her arrival.

I sensed something was wrong. I think I even knew it was Bess and when Mum dashed indoors to grab her car keys, I was there waiting for her. As soon as Mum looked at me she started crying. It confirmed everything.

'Where is she?'

'She's with Dad, in the car. I'm sorry, Emma, I'm so sorry, but there's been an accident. It was the telehandler, it's so heavy, and—' She couldn't say any more.

Tears welled up in my eyes and my throat felt tight and painful. I ran outside and flung myself into the car beside her. Bess lay there in a crumpled heap, her mouth wide open. The only noise coming from her now was a laboured rasp as she breathed in and out.

'Oh,' I said in a trembling voice. I started to shake but took a deep breath and pulled myself together. 'It's OK, Bess, you're going to be fine. I'm coming with you.'

Mum started the car and we set off on the twenty-minute drive to the vet's. I tried to make out in the darkness how badly injured she was. Her crushed back leg hung at a dreadful angle, almost as if it wasn't attached to the rest of her body at all, while her little white paw pointed out to the side. She tried to lift herself up at one point and I could hear her broken bones grind together.

I tried not to think about what would happen when we arrived at the surgery. I didn't want that moment to arrive, yet I also wanted her misery to end as soon as possible. I was not prepared to believe that these

17

were the last minutes I would spend with my best friend Bess.

The journey seemed to take forever, cars ahead of us crawling along as if deliberately trying to slow us down. I could sense Mum getting frustrated in the driver's seat. She kept glancing at me in the rear view mirror; she was as devastated as I was, whether for Bess's sake or for mine I don't know.

When we finally arrived I dashed round to the other side of the car and tried to lift Bess without hurting her. Mum stood beside me, crying quietly as she watched. Despite her pain, Bess made no attempt to snap or growl as I held her in my arms and followed Mum from the dark street into the fluorescent light of the surgery.

I don't know if Mum intended to say it, or if it just came out, but she ignored everything that Dad had said about having Bess put down and greeted the vet with the words, 'Fix this dog. I don't care what it costs, just please fix her.' Huge billowing sobs poured out of her then, as if having relinquished responsibility to someone else she could finally let herself feel the full force of what had happened.

My responsibility, now, was to place Bess on to the examination table as gently as possible. I kept talking to her, reassuring her everything was going to be OK. I remember thinking to myself how brave she was being for me, hiding the extent of the pain behind her dark brown eyes, and how hard I tried to match her courage and hold my emotions in check. When the vet injected her with a painkiller, I watched the needle sink into her fur and the syringe being emptied and felt the relief seep through my whole body.

The vet wanted to muzzle Bess while she examined

her, but I told her that there was no need for that, that I would hold her head steady myself. The vet looked sceptical. For the length of the examination Bess did nothing more than cry a little, and once or twice, when the pain got too much, she licked my arm and looked up at me in confusion.

An X-ray confirmed the worst: she had several fractured vertebrae, her pelvis was broken in several places, her hip joint was shattered and the damage to her leg looked irreparable.

The vet spoke frankly and sympathetically. It would be expensive to operate, she said. It was a dangerous procedure with a severe risk of massive internal bleeding. Even if surgery was a complete success, it would leave Bess lame for the rest of her life. There was one other option—we could say our goodbyes now and let her go.

I stroked Bess's head. I could not look at Mum, but I didn't have to. If Mum hesitated in giving the vet our response, it was only for a second. 'Just do whatever you can.'

The vet nodded.

As they wheeled Bess away her eyes searched for me until the theatre doors flapped shut and she was gone. Then it was my turn to cry. I thought I would never be able to stop.

*   *   *

Bess's recovery was truly remarkable. Youth was on her side, though—her broken leg was pinned and plated and the shattered hip joint removed, but she was strong and otherwise healthy and she healed quickly.

The biggest hardship was the enforced cage rest

she had to endure to ensure that her pelvis healed correctly. Caging a nine-month-old collie is no joke, but Bess was a fine patient. During those four weeks of incarceration the staff at the surgery grew attached to her and, not being able to visit as often as I would have liked, I worried, like a typical thirteen-year-old, that with all these new admirers there to lavish her with care and attention she would soon forget about me. I need not have been so insecure and doubting of her loyalty. Every time I showed up, she was overjoyed to see me.

We all missed having Bess around, and on the day she came home, Mum declared that from now on she would be a house pet, hairs and mess be damned. Bess has lived in Muirfield farmhouse from that day, commandeering her favourite spot on the living room sofa and no other creature—human or beast—would dare claim it from her. Even Dad who, astonishingly, I have witnessed giving up his place so that Bess can make herself comfortable.

I sometimes wonder if my life would have followed a different course if Bess had been put down that night. I think I would have been so sickened that I would never have wanted another dog. Rudyard Kipling once said, 'Beware of giving your heart to a dog to tear.' It is so true: when you take on a dog to love, you make yourself vulnerable to so much heartbreak.

Chapter Two

One rainy night a few days after ringing the National Trust, a large envelope is lying on the mat when I get home from work. The brochure on Fallowlees has arrived. I am cold and wet and was thinking only of lighting the fire, putting the kettle on and running a hot bath, but the moment I see the letter I forget all about that in my haste to rip it open. My hands are trembling—and not from the chill, either.

The photograph on the first page shows a sturdy farmhouse standing beside a mismatch of other stone buildings, sheltering behind three huge sycamore trees. In the foreground, black cows graze next to woolly white-faced Cheviot ewes in a field scattered with bulrushes and edged with a great stone wall.

It looks beautiful.

The farm is one hundred and twenty acres in total and a map shows how it is split into fields. It seems small compared to the land I am managing at Fairspring, but I know it is more than big enough for someone on their own and just starting out. Someone like me, in other words. I try to be cautious. 'Don't go jumping the gun, Emma,' I tell myself, 'you're so not there yet.'

I read on. The farm has no mains electricity or water and no phone line. Power comes from a diesel generator situated in one of the outbuildings, water from a spring. It is flanked on three sides by the mature forests of Harwood, and it is a four-mile drive along a forestry track to Harwood village which isn't a village so much as a huddle of half a dozen houses.

The farmhouse contains three fairly large bedrooms, a bathroom that is apparently in need of renovation and a kitchen that has recently been damp-proofed and fitted with a new Rayburn that the incoming tenant must purchase from the outgoing tenant (I notice it neglects to mention how much *that* will be).

Then comes more detailed information about the ground and the land. I skim through until I come to the part about the sort of candidate the National Trust is looking for. It seems that the farm on its own cannot support anyone, and the prospective candidate must therefore have an alternative income. No problem there as I've no desire to leave Fairspring. As well as earning their own living, the right person will be enthusiastic, highly motivated and able to take care of the farm in an environmentally responsible manner.

That's me! Something feels right about this, like it was *meant to be*. ('You're not there yet, you're not there yet . . .')

I sober up a bit when I read about the application details. It involves having to submit a business plan, a capital budget, three years' profit and loss and three years' cash flow, as well as two references and a letter from my bank. It sounds like a lot of work, daunting work, and doubts start to creep in until I get a grip and tell myself to stop being such a wuss. I needed a challenge and I have found myself a good one—I'm damned if I will let a measly bit of paperwork put me off.

Suddenly I realise that I am shivering. I'm still sitting in a wet coat and the fire remains unlit. I have to go back outside in the rain to collect some logs and coal from the garden. There is a dark art to fire lighting, and to my great frustration I have yet to master it.

Maybe I never will, but I know one thing for sure—*this* particular fire is a complete bastard. Lately I have started to think I imagined the duvet-cosiness that seduced me the first time I visited because no matter what I feed it, the useless thing does a feeble impression of a fire before sighing, shrugging and giving up. I don't know why I bother, but this evening I prepare a bed of squashed-up newspaper, neatly position the fire lighters, lay out the logs and coal, and put a match to it. The fire blazes for all of twenty minutes before slumping to a low glow. All the heat seems to disappear up the chimney. After a bite to eat I decide that rather than faff about getting covered in soot I will take a hot-water bottle to bed and snuggle up with the particulars.

As I settle down with the pages in my chilly attic room, the rain drums on the roof near my head and I feel almost drunkenly contented. I don't know what's got into me, but I seem to have pinned my hopes on this place that I know so little about. Maybe I am looking for a way to dig myself out of the rut I'm in, maybe it is sheer desperation, I don't know, but I picture myself as Emma Gray, the farmer of Fallowlees, and wiggle my toes in delight.

*   *   *

I know better than most that life on a farm is no bed of roses. I have wanted to be a farmer for as long as I can remember, but there have been plenty of times when I've wished I wanted to do something else—anything else—other than follow my father and grandfather into the business. Having said that, I remember my childhood fondly. It was a happy time; the sun always seemed to be shining and there was never a dull moment. Growing up, the eldest of three girls, I was the bossy one, the one who made the decisions and led the mayhem. Whenever disagreements arose between us, I would be prosecution and defence, judge and jury. I was the leader of the pack, protector and defender of my sisters Caroline and Elizabeth, three and seven years my juniors. Mostly, though, I think I was a pain in the backside!

We tussled and argued, played tig, hide and seek; took each other inside to patch up cuts and bruises and back out again minutes later to find more mischief. We had acres to run around in, rows and rows of freshly mown hay to jump over when we had our races. We had fields and fields of long grass to search for four-leaf clovers. One of our favourite tricks was to lie in the grass in the middle of a field of cattle. Cattle are curious creatures, especially young heifers and bullocks, and before long they would make tentative steps towards us, urging each other on until they were licking our wellies and sniffing at our hair. Then all three of us would jump up and shout, 'Boo!' and the cattle would gallop off in mock panic, tossing their heads in the air and arching their tails over their backs, snorting with excitement. Eventually they would pull themselves up, turn round, and the game would begin again. We placed bets on which one would reach us first. We grew up feeling comfortable around animals. They were part of the daily fabric of our lives and they offered us girls the opportunity to be wild things ourselves!

My love of animals extended to adopting lost causes and trying to rehabilitate them. I remember when myxomatosis was epidemic amongst rabbits. I would carry home the listless, malnourished specimens with their gummy eyes, bring them indoors and try to tempt them back to health with carrots and hay, begging them to pull through. Then I remember the heartbreak when, inevitably, they died.

One day I was clambering around in the rafters of one of the outbuildings and discovered a nest containing a single, stone-cold egg. I assumed that the mother bird had abandoned it, so I carefully carried it into our warm kitchen where I wrapped it in toilet roll and placed it in a bowl on the Aga to warm up. I then sat back and waited for the hatching to commence. What sort of bird might it be, I wondered. Wouldn't it be brilliant if it were an owl, or even a dove! I was as proud as any prospective mother.

When Mum walked into the room she took one look at it and yelled, 'Get it out of my kitchen! It'll be rotten!'

I grabbed the nest/bowl and headed for the door but I wasn't quick enough. I had moved all of three paces before the egg exploded with a surprisingly loud *bang!* coating me, the walls and various plates and utensils in a rank and shivering substance the thought of which can still make my stomach turn. I was not particularly popular that night. It took a good few days to wash the persistent pong out of my hair and it was generally agreed that it served me right, as well.

Dad taught me how to make halters for the sheep and I would replicate them on a smaller scale for our two pet lambs. We named them Jumbo and Mouse. Jumbo was a black Leicester and Mouse a squat little Texel. We would race them up and down the yard and take them on long rambling walks during which the pair happily munched the hedgerows as we girls dawdled along behind.

As I grew older there were times when I felt a bit isolated not living in a town, and that I didn't really fit in at school. I seem to remember frayed tempers and my pleas for lifts to and fro, but I think I knew even then that it was a small price to pay for the benefits that farm life had to offer.

I often wonder what my life might have been like if I'd had a brother, whether I would have chosen a different profession and let him get on with the farm work. I might at least have had nice nails and neat hair and not developed a corned beef complexion! I am sure, deep down, that Dad would have liked a son to drive tractors and share the heavier jobs with, someone to pass the family business on to. Perhaps all these years I have been trying to fit that role

I reckon I would have been a brilliant boy!

*   *   *

In March 2001, foot and mouth disease struck the farm. Our entire stock had to be culled. I was fifteen years old and my shiny-happy world came crashing down. Gathering in the ewes and lambs for slaughter was a painful task. Mum wanted us girls to be as little involved as possible, but I was the only one Bess would work for—she was still our best working dog, despite her accident—and so it would be down to us—me and her—to round up the herd for the Army, who had been called in by the Government to complete the cull. It was made particularly tough as we were right in the middle of lambing. It was less than a day's work, and devastating in any number of cruel, senseless ways.

Devastating to see Mum and Dad watch the flock

they had worked so hard to build up destroyed within hours.

Devastating to watch Jumbo and Mouse and their newborn lambs being led away to their sorry fate.

Devastating to know all the while that each tiny newborn would receive a fatal injection to the heart and each adult, my beloved pet sheep among them, would be shot in the head.

Devastating to see hundreds of carcasses removed to a landfill site and dumped, job done.

The farm was tragically empty for nearly a full year afterwards. The tracks worn into the hills by generations of grazing sheep became overgrown for the first time anyone could remember. It sounds like a cliché, but a silence actually fell, hard, over the land and my whole family. We each felt it differently and we all bore it as best we could. As we watched the grass grow high and our spirits wither, farming seemed like the most unrewarding work in the world.

Even Bess took the cull badly and after a few months with no sheep work to occupy her, she took to running off and chasing after other people's dogs when we went to agility practice. We were all grateful when new sheep arrived from an island in Scotland. They started to revive the fields. They gave the farm a reason to resume its familiar routine, getting us back to something that felt 'normal'. Even so, it would take time and a lot of hard work to get these new animals accustomed to the conditions on our land. It was not at all plain sailing.

Around this time, I paid a visit to another farm with Kate, my best friend from high school, and came across a young collie tied to a dilapidated old kennel. He was so happy to see us that he shot forwards, forgetting the chain that tethered him. It

27

yanked him back sharply. As we got closer it became clear that his heavy coat was matted and his tail was so soiled that it stuck to his back legs. Yet despite his distressing condition he was instantly friendly and excessively grateful for the attention we were showing him. I asked the shepherd what the poor mutt was doing there. He was a reject, explained the man, palmed off on them by a family who no longer wanted him, about as useful as a chocolate fireguard and he planned to drown the blighter as soon as he had a spare minute. I was shocked at how blasé he was about it.

'I'll save you the bother,' I replied. 'I'll take him home with me.'

Another of my hopeless cases. We called him Bill. Once again, Dad wasn't over the moon but since Bess had proved to be such a useful sheepdog he had mellowed on the whole dog score. Bill was mainly black, big and shaggy with a solid frame and honest dark eyes. As it turned out he was not such a hopeless case at all. Sure, he could be a bit stupid at times and was too heavy to ever be very fast on his feet, but he was a keen learner, and before long he had joined me and Bess in our agility competing circle.

By the time I was seventeen, all I knew was that I wanted to work with animals, preferably dogs. I had toyed with the idea of studying animal behaviour but couldn't see a real job at the end of it. Then I discovered a residential course in Northumberland specialising in sheep management, the only one of its kind in the country. The clincher was that the student was expected to take along a young Border collie to train. I packed my bags and arrived at Kirkley Hall on the outskirts of Ponteland, Bill in tow.

It was my first time away from home and I loved

it. I became totally caught up in the whirlwind of lectures, studying, training Bill and socialising, so much so that I didn't go back to Hawick as much as I should have done. After all the years I had spent at school feeling 'different', it was amazing to find myself among an entire intake of people my age who came from similar backgrounds, who shared my passions and with whom I shared many—many—bottles of wine. I had never had so much fun. At the weekend I would work on my uncle's farm nearby to earn a little extra cash, most of which I spent in the pub.

Bill kept improving. He would never have the finesse of Bess but when it came to pushing sheep up in the pens none could rival him. I could do the job of three men if I had Bill with me so he became my right-hand man. Meanwhile, Bess was at home on the farm where, since I had been away, she was starting to work pretty well for Mum.

In 2004, straight out of college I travelled to New Zealand for six months to broaden my farming knowledge and my horizons. My eyes had been opened to a world beyond my parents' farm, and I was hungry to explore further. I didn't spare much of a thought for poor Bill or Bess at home with Mum and Dad, nor Mum and Dad for that matter. I was too much in love with my newfound freedom. I was eighteen and it was the first time I had been abroad. An aunt met me at the airport and soon enough I found a job on a pig farm, working as part of a big team. The sheer number of colleagues was a new and fulfilling experience for me, and I adored the pigs—just like the collies, they were such characters. At my interview, my employer had asked me what I knew about them.

'They oink and have curly tails,' I said.

I couldn't have been more wrong. In all the time I was there I never heard a pig oink. They bark, they grunt and they squeal; but they do *not* oink. And as for the curly tails—really, it's too weird—these are chopped off when they are born, kind of like the Three Little Pigs meet the Three Blind Mice.

I was responsible for the farrowing of the main herd and having worked with sheep for so long it was plain sailing as pigs rarely have problems giving birth.

Pigs are vocally very astute creatures and you can almost have a conversation with them. Which I did, often.

'Do you want your breakfast?'

'Arf bark arf.'

'Are you sure?'

'Arf arf, bark bark.'

'OK then, here it is—come and get it!'

'Arf arf, grumble grumble,' followed by contented chomping, gobbling and general scoffing noises.

I came back from New Zealand with a renewed interest in farming.

*   *   *

Viewing day for Fallowlees arrives in early November. I'm beyond excited. I also have a stinking cold. Oh, great. I know I need to dress to impress, because the National Trust agents will be there, but it isn't as easy as it should be. How to look smart and pulled-together and still manage to convince them that I am capable of running a farm?

I wonder how many people will be there. It is quite remote, so perhaps no one else will turn up. Perhaps

30

they will have to beg me to take it on! God, I feel as if I'm on a date. That same fluttery feeling.

I am keen to get Mum and Dad's opinion on the place, and I have arranged to meet them near Fallowlees so that we can look around the farm together. As I drive, I move from main road to back road to lesser-used back road until finally I am on a narrow lane that brings me to the edge of Harwood Forest. A sign indicates the hamlet of Harwood lies straight ahead, through the trees, though it hardly looks as if there could be much human life around here at all . . . Mum and Dad are waiting for me, parked up by the side of the road. I stop my car and hop in to join them in the pickup and together we turn off the lane and head into the forest.

Now we are travelling along a shingle track, only really suited to the forestry wagons that work here. Huge forty-year-old spruce trees stand to attention on each side, like a guard of honour. We make a note of the mileage to see how far from the road the farm is. It's a bit like going through a maze. All the trees look identical and there are no landmarks. Luckily the National Trust has put up signs to help us. The track gets worse as we progress, made so rough with potholes and large cobbles as to render it treacherous for any less sturdy vehicles. After about two miles we come across a house. I can see instantly that this neglected place is not Fallowlees, but it is shown on the map as Redpath. Along with the adjoining land, Redpath is part of the tenancy. It is large and well built, the roof is sound—it is not derelict by any means—but it is long-since abandoned. Grass is growing in the gutters and weeds are sprouting up in the doorway and on the windowsills. The front door is open and swinging in the breeze. I can so

31

easily picture it full of people, as the busy working farm and family home it must once have been. Now it is a forlorn thing, staring at the wildwood with wide window-eyes and yet somehow the fact that it belongs to the farm makes my heart race.

As we carry on along the track we are flanked by trees at different stages of growth, from slender saplings to mighty sky-skimmers. Every now and then, a smattering of hardwood or a stand of Scots pine breaks the monotony. At last, Fallowlees comes into view. According to the milometer we have only travelled four or so miles, and it has taken us nearly twenty minutes to get that far. I would be grumbling about it by now, but the sight of the farm has dissolved all negativity.

Fallowlees is as pretty as it was in the brochure. Prettier.

'Just look at all the cars!' says Mum, dragging me back to earth as ever.

There are cars on both sides of the road leading up to the house, cars in the drive, and even a car in the field. There must be almost thirty. Dad *harrumphs* his astonishment. I slump back in my seat, speechless, trying to process the extent of the competition and my wafer-thin chance of winning.

I am already hopelessly smitten and now I feel like a plain-faced wannabe in love with some handsome leading man, knowing that amid a host of glittering stars she will only get the bit part, never the romantic lead. I am such an unlikely prospect on several counts. I am twenty-three years old, which is young for anyone to have a farm; I am single, which I know will be seen as a distinct disadvantage living out here in the wilds; but perhaps the biggest barrier of all is my gender. I have never been blind to the fact that as a woman in a man's world, I will have to face some tough knockbacks: I just had not prepared myself for this to be one of them.

Dad notices the change in my body language and he gives me a good talking-to. 'You're just as good as anyone else here. You stand an equally good chance. Now pull yourself together and let's do what we came here to do.'

I try telling him I'm not being a pessimist, just realistic, but he doesn't even deem this worthy of a reply. As we make our way across the yard I watch a young couple enthusing over the buildings. They look such ideal tenants! A middle-aged man and woman with a teenage son are walking through one of the fields and looking as if they belong there. A woman walks out of the farmhouse alone, but is followed ten seconds later by her husband holding the baby. From the conversation I overhear, it sounds as if they're already making plans for moving in. Everyone else here seems so promising!

'It's all couples,' I mutter to Mum and Dad, but they take no notice.

One of the National Trust agents introduces himself as Julian and we all shake hands. He asks Dad what he thinks about the place and Dad, nodding towards me, says, 'Not me you should be asking.' I expect Julian to be surprised, but he doesn't appear to be. He asks me what I'm doing now and what my plans are for the farm. His interest makes me feel a bit more hopeful and I decide to make an effort after all.

We leave Julian and head for the farmhouse, but it is chock-a-block with people and as all the National Trust agents inside seem to be cornered, we decide to explore outside first. The first field is not quite moorland, but it is not far off; it's a bit wet after the recent rainfall but still looks good. The three small fields close to the house are almost like meadows, but behind them the soil is poorer, with rushes and weeds growing all over the place. The current tenant's black Galloway cattle graze gently close by.

'I thought Galloway cattle were supposed to be wild, Dad.'

'Well, all the ones I've ever worked with were,' he replies, and we stand for a while looking at these contented, hairy cows with their flopping fringes and big brown eyes.

The fields are not exactly stock-proof. Even though they are fenced in by big, well-built stone walls, time has taken its toll on the enclosures and great gaps have opened up so that the farm now seems, pretty much, to be run as one large field.

In front of the house is a fantastic field, around seven acres in size, and of all of them this is certainly the most stock-proof. I can just see myself in the middle of it, long lead in my hand, a packet of sheep to practise on, training young dogs.

As we make our way to the steading, Dad manages to step into a bog right up to his knees. Mum and I fall about laughing and Dad eventually sees the funny side though he's pretty miffed as he's wearing his favourite trainers.

Fallowlees Bastle, the ruins of an ancient building and protected by law, lies alongside the outbuildings. Hard to tell how big it was originally but it is an impressive sight even now. The stones are huge, each one weighing more than a grown man. No wonder it has withstood the ravages of time.

We make our way over for a closer inspection of the farm buildings. There is a cattle shed and a large polytunnel, the sort commonly used for growing vegetables, but set up here to provide shelter for sheep at lambing time. There are other sheds, including a timber one housing the generator. Best of all are the three stone byres, still kitted out with the original stalls from the days when every farm made its own butter, milk and cream. Each cow would be chained in a stall to be milked and each stall had two troughs—one for water and one for hay. The woodwork is still intact, worn smooth by generations of cattle brushing up against it.

I am thinking that the byres would make perfect kennels; I have filled them with champion sheepdogs already. For the umpteenth time, I tell myself not to get carried away with forward plans, but I seem to be fighting a losing battle.

Now that some of the people have gone, Mum and I leave Dad outdoors in his mucky state and look around the house. The first thing I notice is the sheer cliff face of stairs that greets us in the hallway. It is the steepest staircase I have ever seen and I'm afraid to say that my first thought is, 'God. I'll have to be careful after a glass of wine!' The master bedroom is bright and airy, filled with golden autumn light. Two huge windows look south across Greenleighton Moor and the view from them is magnificent—wild moorland, untouched, stretching away for miles.

We go back down the precipitous staircase and into the kitchen, which is full of people. The kitchen is the heart in any farmhouse. A green Rayburn underneath a great stone lintel forms the centrepiece of this cosy room, cradled by vast beams. There is a red flagstone floor and the units are wooden and rustic. The walls are a comfy creamy colour that reminds me of newborn lamb fleece; I feel right at home.

It is warmer in here than the rest of the house and the sudden heat makes my nose run. As I rummage for a tissue, I notice a man standing at the window, his face silhouetted. At a smallish round table an agent—'Anna' says her name badge—is standing taking questions on the plans of the farm, which are spread out on the tabletop.

Anna tells us that there is a possibility that Fallowlees will have its own windmill installed in the near future so the generator, which we've heard clanking away outside, will no longer be required. She then introduces me and Mum to the man in the window. Rob is the outgoing tenant, tall and dark and in his thirties. We chat politely about the recent wet weather before we discover that we know some of the same people so we move on to a bit of gossip. Now that the ice is broken I feel much more confident.

As we drive away from Fallowlees, I try and sort through my conflicting feelings. There is absolutely no doubt that I love the place; but the thought of the long and complicated application procedure is still troubling me, even more so now that I have seen the competition. I have never put anything like that together before and I have to wonder if it is really worth all that time and effort when I surely stand such little chance of getting anywhere with it. Dad glances at me in the rear view mirror; it is as if he can hear me think.

'Well?'

'Nothing, Dad. There's just a lot to take in, that's all.'

The journey back to my car seems quicker than the journey up. Mum and Dad get out with me and we stand there looking up and down the little lane, as if expecting it to have sprouted houses and street lamps in our absence.

'Well?' says Dad again.

'It is a beautiful spot,' Mum says quickly, 'but it's a long way from anywhere else. Especially for a young girl.' She eyes me anxiously.

'Rothbury's a few miles that way,' I say, pointing, 'and Otterburn's a few miles over the other way, so it's not really as remote as all that. Just feels like it, that's all.'

Mum doesn't look convinced.

'I'll call you tomorrow. Thanks for coming with me.'

I have already decided that I'm going to go for it. I have nothing to lose after all, apart from hope—and hope is going to be in short supply in any case. I climb back into my pickup and start the engine. If today made me realise anything it is that I can't carry on living the way I am now. If something doesn't change soon I'm going to have to give up my job and move back in with Mum and Dad.

Fallowlees holds the key to that 'other life', the 'more-than-this' life I always sensed was out there for me.

Fallowlees is the reason I left Steven, the reason I took such a risk in the first place.

Fallowlees is my last chance.

Chapter Three

My evenings have changed since I discovered Fallowlees. I no longer dread coming home at the end of a long day. The first thing to do after getting in is make sure the dogs are nice and dry in their kennels; then I tackle that blasted fire and when the water's hot enough I take a quick shower. Then I sit by the fireside, as close as I dare—sometimes actually perching on the hearth—until I am warm through to the bones. All the while, I'll be thinking about my application. Over the days and nights that follow the viewing, I decide how many sheep the farm can carry and I ponder over the benefits of cattle; I work out the cost of insurance, fuel, repairs, equipment .ð.ð. the list goes on and on. It is even more work than I thought, but after a few weeks of research and number crunching I decide it is time to write it all up properly.

Since I don't have a computer I head to the library in Hexham, armed with the great wad of scrap paper I've used for all my notes and workings-out, and book myself some time on a PC. Once I start typing, it isn't long before I am in full flow. I have finished my proposal and two of the annual cash flows and am making a start on the third when I realise that I have not saved any of the three open documents—a good half hour's work. Idiot. Idiot. Idiot. Hastily, I go to name and save them all. Then sod's law kicks in and the computer freezes. My skin starts to sizzle like the desktop's screen-glow static, and my stomach lurches. This is not good. Not good at all. I wait a few seconds, wiggle the mouse around: nothing happens.

With rising panic, I go to find an assistant.

'Oh, that does happen sometimes. I assume you saved what you were doing?' she says as she comes over. I have an overwhelming desire to lash out, shove her hard so she falls against the stacks (preferably into *Computing for Dummies*).

'Let's reboot it, shall we?' I stand behind her, staring desperately at the screen. When it springs back to life, all my work has disappeared.

Tears fill my eyes. The proposal is due in tomorrow and the library closes soon. The thought of doing it all again is just too much to contemplate; this latest calamity only fuels my doubts and insecurities. People have been saying all along that I am wasting my time and clearly I should have listened to them. The farmers at the auction mart went out of their way to instil a note of caution, warning that the National Trust would never give a farm to a twenty-three-year-old or a single person, much less a single twenty-three-year-old *lass* like me. They mean to be kind, but their faces betray them—they see me as a dreamer, a silly impulsive girl who would do well to stick to what she knows best.

They are right, I *am* a dreamer—but this dream of Fallowlees has occupied me ever since Hylton told me about it and has only grown stronger since the visit made it more of a reality. Either I go for it—and face my doubters in a few weeks' time with news of my rejection—or I save myself the effort and any future embarrassment, and walk away. In spite of everything, I can't let it slip away that easily. It's now or never.

Choking back my tears, I return to the screen, open another blank document and save it straight away. I start typing again (hitting 'save' every few

39

lines) and before long my fingers are racing over the keys and I am lost in a trance. I am no longer in the musty library but back in that huge front field with the sun in my eyes, Fly, Bill, Roy and Alfie beside me, all five of us ready to take on anything. I keep typing and saving, typing and saving, until the library is almost empty and the librarians are glancing at their watches. I start to feel self-conscious until, with a shock, I realise that I have finished. I print, pay and file the proposal in a neat little folder ready to take to the National Trust offices before noon the next day.

It is dark when I get outside but as I get back to the pickup, something catches my eye. A parking ticket, slapped under the wipers. I don't know whether it is anger or just all that frustration and anxiety I've been carrying around, but this is the last straw and I burst into tears. I howl it all out; and after a good ten minutes I feel spent, relieved, and very much better. All I want now is to head back to Marlene Cottage and cuddle my dogs.

*   *   *

After handing in my application the next day, I decide a trip home is in order. Dad's helped a lot as I've been putting the proposal together but he hasn't yet seen the result of my labours and I'm keen to show him what I've done. I also feel the need for some home comforts and I load up the dogs and head north for Scotland.

Bill has been staying with my parents since I moved to the cottage and he is the first to welcome us back as I pull up. He woofs hello and goes to find a toy for me to throw. Some things never change, I think

40

with a smile. Mum doesn't bother locking him up as he's such an easy-going character; he just potters round the farm and plays with the other dogs. I am surprised to see the beginnings of a silver film in those dark eyes of his. He's getting old. I throw the toy and he bounds after it like a puppy, just the way he's always done. Like all men, he is just a child at heart.

Bess is sitting under the kitchen table and this time when I greet her she actually gets up and comes over for a pat and a fuss. Things will never be the same as they used to be, but at least we have an understanding now.

Mum puts the kettle on and a few minutes later Dad appears.

'Christ, Emma, you look terrible!'

I'm a bit taken aback. 'That bad, eh?'

'Sorry, but you just don't look yourself. Are you eating healthily? You're not missing breakfast are you?'

Dad and his breakfasts. He firmly believes in the power of the most important meal of the day, and his spreads are legendary. Each one is a carefully constructed masterpiece consisting of a number of components assembled in a very precise recipe. First is the porridge, made with whole milk. Then comes a spoonful of honey, a dollop of Greek yogurt, a generous smattering of fruit muesli, several slices of golden-sweet grapefruit and a final flurry of dark brown sugar. The thought of that lovely bowlful is one of the reasons I hanker for home—like father, like daughter.

I assure Dad that I've been eating well. 'I'm probably just tired,' I say. He and Mum exchange looks and I can see just what they're thinking: you didn't look like that when you and Steven were together.

I've had all this so many times, and I'm about to get annoyed about it when I remember the proposal.

'Don't say anything,' I say, eager to keep the lid on that can of worms, 'and just read this.'

I watch Dad closely as he reads, looking for any hints of what he might be thinking. I always value his and Mum's opinions. He doesn't say a word. When he gets to the end he coughs and says, 'Well done, it's good.'

I blush. It's not like Dad to praise any of us.

'Do you think I'll get an interview?'

'You certainly will with that,' he replies.

Mum isn't so sure, though. 'It depends what they're looking for. You're a single girl, and you're still young, and in any case I'm not sure I like the idea of you all the way out there by yourself.'

I am disappointed by her attitude but I know she is looking out for me; she has always been a worrier where her daughters are concerned. I cannot hold it against her. Certainly not when she has a beautiful welcome-home tea of lamb hotpot and baked potatoes slathered in butter waiting for me. We all sit down to eat together at our huge kitchen table. My sister Lizzy is with us but Caroline is away at university.

Mum looks at us all and sighs. 'We never have all three of you girls together any more.'

*   *   *

After we've eaten I take the dogs for a walk along the track that runs through the farm. Bill trots happily along with us, as I thought he might, and Bess decides to come, too, which is more of a

42

surprise. It's dark, but it doesn't bother me. I know this road like the back of my hand; I've walked it for as long as I can remember. As my eyes adjust, I can make out the different forms of the dogs snuffling about in the verges. Bill is bumping around with what looks like the bough of a tree in his mouth, whacking the other dogs with it if they get too close. They don't seem to mind. I envy them their contentment. They have nothing to worry about, they live for the moment and I am there to provide for them. As for me, I'm always thinking ahead, worrying about what the future might bring. I'm becoming more and more convinced that Fallowlees is my last chance. I can't see Marlene Cottage as anything other than a temporary measure; the dogs are not suited to living in a backyard and apart from that I want to be back on a farm. Village life isn't all it's cracked up to be when your heart is somewhere else.

I put the dogs away and join Mum and Dad for a glass of wine. In the warmth of the farmhouse, with the people I love around me, I reflect that if things don't go my way with Fallowlees, being home wouldn't be such a bad thing.

* * *

Fairspring Farm belongs to Ken Pickering and Hilary Ross. They have owned it for many years and farmed it themselves until the foot and mouth crisis of 2001. When that was over they decided that rather than starting again from scratch they would let it out to a local farmer, Michael Suddes. It's Michael I work for.

Michael is a great boss. He is principally an arable

43

farmer and runs a large farm of his own a few miles away. He took on Fairspring as a bit of a side venture, renting just a few sheds at first, and then taking over a large part of the farm when Ken and Hilary lost all their stock. By the time I had been there a year, he was renting Fairspring in its entirety.

Michael is himself a very good stockperson, and at lambing time you will find no better helping hand; but he is wise and knows his staff well. He leaves me to my own devices, and that is exactly how I like it. I pride myself on my independence and like to do things my own way with just my dogs to help me.

Ken and Hilary are great, too. Ken pretends to be a grumpy old man but he has a heart of gold. He loves to take the mick out of people, and those who can't learn to laugh it off and give as good as they get inevitably end up feeling horribly offended. There are times when I am the bane of Ken's life since I am notoriously clumsy and accident prone, and he is responsible for repairs. Ken can do a marvellous imitation of me in a Scottish accent, 'It just happened!' And it so often does. The gates fall off in my hands, the bike gets itself stuck, the rails in the sheep pens somehow break. The list is exhausting, and poor Ken has to follow my trail of devastation, fixing as he goes.

Hilary took early retirement from her veterinary practice to pursue a career in athletics and she has become the world triathlon champion in her age category. She is possibly one of the most dedicated people I will ever meet. Even when she was working full-time, she was out training at first light whatever the weather, pounding the country roads or putting her bike through its paces. She is tiny, built like a whippet, and is blessed with one of the sharpest brains in the business.

I count myself lucky to work at Fairspring. And as I go about my work over the next few days, the thought of that farm in the forest makes me smile even more than usual.

*　　　*　　　*

The letter from the National Trust is lying on my doormat. I look at it nervously, pick it up, finger it carefully, trying to gauge whether its size might give me a clue as to its contents. It feels like a single sheet of paper. I take a deep breath, rip it open and . . . I have made it through to interview!

A brief moment of giddy glee involving jumping up and down and dancing around like a demented bunny rabbit is followed immediately by thoughts of my wardrobe: I will need something to wear. It is very rare indeed for me to be seen in anything other than tracksuit bottoms or jeans. The dressier outfits I own, for nights out with the girls, are hardly suitable for the most important interview of my life. In the end, I borrow a pair of black trousers and a white shirt from Mum. The shirt is slightly too large and a bit see-through but I cover it up with a rather smart jacket I didn't even know I had (I found it lurking in my wardrobe, never worn once) and slip on a pair of flat black shoes—and that's me, smartened up and ready for anything . . . isn't it?

I look in the mirror and a not-quite-right version of me stares back. I feel all wrong. I wear make-up every day for work. I may spend most of my time up to my knees in muck, and smelling of farmyard, but I do want to keep *some* sense of femininity. When it comes to the interview, however, I haven't bothered.

I thought the panel might take me more seriously without anything frivolous and girly like make-up. Instead, I just look tired and terrible. I smooth my skin with a smudge of foundation, open up my eyes with a sweep or two of mascara, finish off with a lick of colour to my lips, and instantly look and feel miles better. With a copy of my proposal under my arm, I am on my way.

*   *   *

The National Trust offices are in the village of Scots Gap. As I climb out of the pickup I manage to get a dirty mark on my jacket. Great start. I steel myself, rub it clean as best I can, and head for the entrance. *Don't blow it*, a voice inside me is saying.

The waiting room is hot but I don't dare take off my jacket because of the sheerness of the blouse. When I sit down my trousers ride up my shins, exposing my horrible shoes and odd socks. I feel ridiculous. I must have read my proposal about a hundred times but suddenly I have no idea what on earth is in it.

I'm considering looking through it yet again when a familiar face appears to greet me. It's Anna, the agent I met at Fallowlees, and I follow her through the corridors to the interview room. Her pleasant welcome has helped to steady my nerves although as I walk into the room I feel my heart starting to beat harder.

Inside is a large table with three seats on one side and one on the other. I shake hands with each member of the panel, remembering that a firm handshake creates a good impression. Rob Dyson, the outgoing tenant, smiles warmly but in his suit and tie looks almost unrecognisable from the man I met on viewing day. It's a bit disconcerting. A dark-haired woman in her forties is another National Trust employee. Anna sits down between them. She is one of those people who always look immaculate—cool, blonde and efficient. As for me, my face must be hot enough to fry an egg on.

I sit down opposite them and immediately become more conscious of my hands than I have ever been: what should I do with them? It feels more efficient to put them on the table, but the table is very high—too high—and as soon as I've placed them there I wish I hadn't. I feel like a child. I can't move them now! I'll only draw attention to the awkwardness. God. What's wrong with me! I leave them where they are. We each have a glass of water in front of us and there is a large decanter in the centre of the table.

'Eeh, it's just like being on the *Apprentice*,' I joke. They laugh. They're probably just being polite but I feel a bit more at ease.

The interview starts with Rob reading out some standard questions from the National Trust. Most of them are about cross compliance, which is the farmer demonstrating good agricultural and environmental practice. I answer questions about native wildlife, ground-nesting birds, the times of year not to mow fields or trim hedges. He wonders what I know about the National Trust and its work and I answer with a degree of confidence. I've been swotting up on that. So far, I've been in my comfort zone. Next it's Anna's turn. She has my proposal in front of her and she looks down at it, pauses for a few seconds, then fixes her blue eyes on me and says that she liked it very much. I think my heart will pound out of my chest and land on the table in front of us. She asks about some of the figures, and I find myself giving good, comprehensive answers as I explain my business plan more fully. Anna nods her head as I talk, and seems satisfied with my responses.

The woman beside her asks me some more general questions about myself and how I would cope with the isolation. These questions are hardly a surprise and I'm prepared for them. I know it's no good being defensive about concerns over my youth or my sex. Instead I tell the panel that farming as an occupation always provides a degree of isolation, and that I have been used to that all my life. It is only now, living in a village for the first time ever, that I am experiencing loneliness. In reality, I say with some conviction, I will be no more isolated than any person who lives on their own, and in many ways I will be less so as I have my dogs and I am used to my own company. A life that draws on my resourceful nature will be far better for me than my unsatisfactory current existence.

All three of them are looking at me closely. My questioner nods thoughtfully and makes a few notes. I wish I knew what she was writing.

As the interview comes to an end they ask me if there is anything I would like to add. I have been waiting for this. I tell them how Michael, recognising my keenness, bought another six hundred sheep in order to keep me at Fairspring Farm, and how I run the flock myself. Then, sounding rather like Elizabeth I addressing her men before the threat of the Spanish Armada, I say that I may be slightly built, single and still young in some people's eyes, but what I lack in age, status and stature—I will make no apology for my sex—I compensate for with enthusiasm and sheer guts. Inside, I have a core of steel. If you let me have this farm, I plead, lifting my

48

hands from the table and clasping them together, I will put my heart and soul into it. You will not regret putting your faith in me.

A slight smile flickers on Anna's lips. Have I gone a bit over the top? There is a fine line between confidence and cockiness. Rob is smiling, too, but all they do is thank me very much for coming in and say that they'll be in touch soon.

I go back to my pickup feeling deflated—all that preparation, all the build-up, and the decision could all hang on a few words. I turn my phone back on and Dad calls seconds later. He asks how it went and I tell him as much as I can remember. Dad is sure I'm going to get it. I wish I had his optimism.

*   *   *

Today is raddle day. The tups have been out with the ewes for seventeen days, which is the length of a ewe's menstrual cycle, so I would expect most of the ewes to be in lamb. It is time to gather in all the tups and rub a thick, oily dye called 'raddle' on to their chests. This means that any ewe that they mount from now on will be marked with a colour (in this case blue) on their rumps and I will be able to tell which ewes will be later to lamb and will not need to come into the shed quite as early.

The tups have had the time of their lives and will have already served more than fifty ewes each. They have been working so hard and eating so little that they are getting a bit scraggy, but they are as stubborn as ever. Because of that I decide to use Roy to gather them in. Roy is the toughest dog I have ever owned. He has never taken a backward step from a sheep in his life and I know that the tups will give him no problem; they know him well and more than one has taken a sharp bite to the nose for daring to disobey him.

I cast him out round the first field and by the time the flock have reached my feet the five tups are already at the back. I make a split in the flock and Roy shoots in and cuts off the tups and a handful of ewes that must be in season and so are loath to leave their men. We walk them into the pens; Roy has made it look easy.

I mix blue powder with oil until it is thickened and gloopy, ready to apply it to their chests using a stick. Each tup weighs at least one hundred kilograms and is frighteningly strong. As I plan my method of attack, I hear someone say hello and am pleased to see Archie making his way across the pens.

'Hey, you're just who I need to help me get the colour on to these boys!'

Archie is in his mid-seventies and retired, with no sheep of his own. We first met at a dog trial. I watched him handling his big rough-coated collie, Dale, flawlessly round the course, gently pushing the sheep where they needed to be, all control and power. Later, when I congratulated him on his run, he simply shook his head and protested that it should have been better. He told me he liked to keep his hand in but that meant relying on the hospitality of farmers and he wasn't one to impose on anyone's good nature.

'Well, I've got loads of sheep and you're more than welcome to run on them any time,' I said. 'In fact, it would be great if you could come on some of the gathers.'

From that moment on, we were friends and Archie would come to the farm every week, sometimes every day if it was busy. He was tough in the way only lifelong farmers can be. He had suffered a heart attack while training a keen young dog the previous year but had made a remarkable recovery so I never worried about giving him plenty to do if he wanted it. The visits to the farm seemed to help his collie, Dale, too. Dogs get bored with training and love an excuse to work sheep properly. I watched him grow fitter by the day.

There's not much Archie doesn't know about training sheepdogs and I am always picking his brains. At trials he is my biggest supporter as well as my biggest critic. He is the first to congratulate me after a good run, but the first to scold me if I mess up. 'What do you think you were doing there? You should have done this!'

I'm glad he is here to give me a hand with the tups. We wrestle with the smallest one first, trying to turn him over, and fail miserably. We must be quite a sight, the slightly built girl, the OAP and a great woolly ball of a sheep, and we fall about laughing at our pathetic attempt. This time last year I had Steven to help me but now, as so often happens, I'm having to think of a way round my lack of strength. Archie and I decide that the only solution is for one of us to corner the tup while the other one gets down and applies the colour. It is a messy way of doing it, but it works. By lunchtime, with only one field left, we are both blue from top to toe.

Archie puffs out his cheeks and says it's time to eat and I take no persuading. I let out Fly and Alfie to join Roy, who is recovering from his run-ins with the tups (though I suspect he enjoyed the battle) and Archie lets Dale go and run around with them too. We sit down on the straw bales left over from last

51

lambing time. Archie pulls out his familiar carpetbag full of homemade goodies and pours us both a cup of tea as we munch our sandwiches.

He asks me about Fallowlees and how the interview went and it feels good to talk to someone about it who has faith in my abilities, who I know is not going to laugh at me. I tell him that although the interview went well, I am not so confident about it now. I think the panel must have seen more suitable candidates.

'Divvent talk daft,' he says in his thick Northumberland accent. 'You've as good a chance as any of them. Mebbes even better.'

'You reckon?'

'Aye. Sounds to me like a place for a youngster, someone with plenty o' fresh ideas and no ties to drag them down.'

'I hope you're right, Archie. Do you know what the word "Fallowlees" actually means? It's such a lovely name.'

Archie is a bit of an oracle on things like this and I am not surprised that he has a ready answer. 'Well, *fallow* can mean "sheltered" and *lee* means "to the side of".'

'So it means "beside sheltered land". I like that.'

Archie grins. 'Well now, *fallow* has another meaning, too.'

'What's that?'

'It also means "useless".'

'Well that's just perfect. With my luck, I know which one's the more likely.'

We both have a good old chuckle then go back to raddling the tups.

*　　　*　　　*

A few days later Anna calls from the National Trust to tell me that there are two main contenders for the farm and I am one of them. I try not to squeal with excitement. She asks if there is any chance I can meet her at Fallowlees the next day to discuss a few issues. I agree in a flash and put the phone down feeling elated.

The following day, Anna greets me with a smile and a handshake and we go inside. The house echoes to our voices now that Rob's furniture has gone. The kitchen is cold. Anna lays the paperwork out on the bench and we go through it together. At the end she straightens up, looks me in the eye, and tells me that, actually, I am their favourite candidate but they will need more rent. This is worrying news as I feel I've already offered as much as I can afford, and it's not as if I'm going to be able to make much from Fallowlees. Anna is sympathetic, we talk through all the options and in the end I agree to carry out a six-hundred-metre stretch of fencing around Redpath in lieu of payment.

'Well, I think we've got a deal,' she says.

'Er, yes, thank you.' Is that really it?

Anna holds out her manicured hand. I take it in mine—too giddy to be embarrassed by my stumpy nails and rough skin—and shake it like I'm mixing a cocktail, before she can change her mind. I am a fully-fledged farmer!

The first thing I do is ring home to tell Mum and Dad. Mum is happy but still a bit cautious. Dad, on the other hand, is bursting with unreserved pride; he tells me that he got the tenancy of Muirfield at the same age, when he was just twenty-three.

I stay behind on the farm after Anna leaves. *My* farm. I walk around the sheds and touch the stonework and the timber. I stride through the fields. I breathe it all in: the emptiness, the views, the sharp fresh air, even the history—a history that I am now a part of.

I can't wait to see the faces of all those cynics! They won't believe it. *I* can't believe it. I keep thinking that something is going to happen to ruin it, as if perhaps I am just a schmuck in an ill-judged episode of *You've Been Framed*. But no; I am alone, just me. I look up at the birds flying loops in the sky above me. I am Emma Gray, I am twenty-three years old and I am the farmer of Fallowlees.

I want to shout and tell the world, but instead I drive quietly through the forest, back to Marlene Cottage and the dogs. I tell them all about the great life they are going to have, all the acres they will have to roam on, all the sheep they will have to play with. Roy and Alfie seem rather unconcerned although they sense my relief and dart around excitedly. Fly, however, looks at me with her head on one side, one ear up and one down, and I could swear she understands.

Chapter Four

Fallowlees is officially in my care from the start of the new year, but as Rob and his wife Caroline have already left for their new farm, I am allowed to start moving my stuff over in late November. I am really busy shepherding my ewes, but I often find my mind straying to that sandstone farmhouse in Harwood Forest. The picture book setting in the trees is ready made for Christmas celebrations.

Things seem so much better now. I am still at Marlene Cottage but I no longer mind the chill; the thought of my imminent move makes up for any discomfort. Only now do I realise how hopeless my life has felt in the months since leaving Steven.

I find myself literally counting down the days.

The start of December brings the first frost. A couple of days later I wake up one morning and wonder why it is so dark. I check my clock. It doesn't make sense. I get up and cross to the window. Nearly a foot of snow has fallen overnight, and it is still falling. A thick layer covers the glass, blocking out the light, while outside ponderous clouds hang in the sky. The village looks beautiful under its blanket of purest white, but to me it spells potential disaster. The sheep are at that critical stage of gestation when the body can terminate the pregnancy or reabsorb the foetus if it feels that its nutrition is not good enough or if the ewe is under too much stress. I have to get to Fairspring, no matter what, to get some fodder out for them. The precious energy they are using to dig out the grass could be greater than what they will recoup from feeding on it.

I have a very quick breakfast, look at my scruffy pickup, and say to it, 'Right, it's you and me now, do not even think about letting me down.'

I load up the three dogs but we hit a snag before we even get going: the driveway is blocked. Even with the vehicle in four-wheel-drive mode, it can't negotiate it. I have to get out and dig a path and it is about forty-five minutes until we are finally on the road. Or what I think must be the road. I must be the first to try to get out of the village. The snow has obliterated all landmarks and I just have to guess where it might be and hope I don't meet any other traffic.

I follow the single track, concentrating deeply on my driving. Every so often I come across mountainous snowdrifts and have to reverse and hit them flat out in order to break through. I hope it doesn't get any worse while I'm out as I know the gritter is unlikely to get here for a few days.

It is a huge relief to make it to the farm. It is deathly quiet. The whole world seems a more silent place in the snow. I start up the telehandler—practically the same model as the one that ran over Bess that awful night—and spear one of the bales of stored feed we call haylage, then set off with it for the first field.

Usually I would expect to find the sheep scattered in ones and twos around the field, but today they are waiting for me huddled together near the gate. They may have smelled the fodder on its way. I cast a quick eye over them. They look well, although the tups appear to be slightly the worse for wear after being active for so long. They stand in their own group, the rivalries of the start of the season long forgotten. The fact that they are together like this is a sign that they have done their job and that nearly all the ewes are pregnant.

Only a few of these ewes have the blue markings, indicating that most got pregnant in the first seventeen days they were with the tups. It's going to be a fast lambing.

The ewes follow me from a short distance away. They know that the telehandler brings good things. I stop next to a feeder and lower the bale on the front of the machine. I hop out and make a few slashes with my pocketknife to tear a hole in the black plastic and reveal the haylage. I jump back into the cabin and, with a flick of the joystick, tip the bale into the feeder. Now the hungry ewes move in and start greedily pulling at their food. Satisfied that they will have enough to keep them going for a while, I repeat the procedure in each of the fields until, right at the end of the day as the grey skies turn black, all nine hundred ewes are full and contented.

It gets dark so early now, and I dread the drive home. More snow has fallen and the tracks I made earlier have practically disappeared. I drive gingerly, and I feel more relieved to see the village lights glowing through the gloom than I have since I first moved in. The dogs' runs are full of snow and I decide to walk them and let them spend the night in the back of the pickup as it is warmly bedded with straw and blankets.

I half expect the snow to be gone in a day or two. Even here in north-eastern England it doesn't usually settle for long, except on high ground—but this year is different. It snows, it snows some more, and it carries on snowing. It lies on the ground for weeks, freezes over, is covered with new snowfall, which freezes over again; and it continues like this, like an elaborate layer cake. Christmas gets closer and I realise that I haven't seen a blade of grass for weeks. We have never known anything like it and the snow has become the main topic of conversation on the streets, on the radio, on television, and it is the same all through the country. Roads are impassable; schools, shops and public buildings are closed; people are prisoners in their own homes.

Not me. I can't sit back and wait for it to go. Nine hundred sheep are relying on my daily visits. Never have they needed me more. They remain in their groups, never straying far from the feeders, and when they are not eating, they are either sleeping or chewing cud, saving their energy. They will need it as their pregnancies progress.

*   *   *

I have not seen Fallowlees since the day I shook hands with Anna. I want so much to be there but I have had to accept that it isn't going to happen for some time yet. It just isn't practical or safe; but one Saturday, just before Christmas, I decide—what the heck!—I am going over there, come what may. It actually looks quite promising outside; instead of the dark snow clouds that have become the norm, it's sunny and bright with hardly a blemish in the sky. I don't tell anyone what I'm up to. They'll only try to dissuade me. Even Archie would probably tell me I was being a bit rash.

I travel the winding roads that lead to the village of Cambo. This is home to the National Trust's Wallington Hall, and the estate to which Fallowlees belongs. The fine country house is a popular tourist attraction and is surrounded by parkland, woodland

and formal gardens which are open all year round though there is no sign of visitors today. As the land rises to the north to Harwood Forest it becomes wilder, suitable only for poorer upland grazing. My new farm is classified as a Less Favoured Area, but that is all part of the challenge for me.

The roads have been ploughed since the first snows—I doubt I would have got this far if I had tried to visit a few weeks ago. Harwood Forest stretches for miles and miles. I can hardly believe I am going to live in the middle of it. I laugh to myself: I will be like Winnie the Pooh in the Hundred Acre Wood! When I enter the forest, the scene that greets me steals my breath. It is as if I'd walked through the wardrobe and into Narnia. The great fir tree boughs bow down, genuflect to the ground under the weight of the snow, their bulk blocking out the low winter sun so that the track fades away into semi-darkness. It is clear that no one has been here for some time, and yet again there are no track marks to follow. I creep up cautiously, my eyes straining at the windscreen. I make it to Redpath. The house looks so beautiful in all its loneliness, but I daren't stop in case I can't get going again. I carry on and eventually Fallowlees appears in the distance. It is the only feature in a monochrome world. The snow is so deep that I can't even make out the boundaries of the drystone wall on the big field.

I sit there gazing at it. I know I risk getting stuck if I go any further, and, reluctantly, after a few minutes the pickup and I follow our own tracks back to the road.

*   *   *

Christmas arrives before I know it. The whole family is excited about my move.

'We might be the ones sitting round *your* table next year, Emma,' says Dad, as we sit down to dinner on Christmas Day, winking at the others. Not likely! One look at my sisters' faces confirms that nobody will want to forsake Mum's cooking for mine.

'I always knew you'd have your own farm, ever since that day you told me not to get up in the morning because you and Bess were going to bring the sheep in.'

Oh no, not that story again. I groan with embarrassment, while Bess, hearing her name, cocks an ear.

'You were about fourteen, remember, and you started giving me a lesson in the finer points of sheepdog handling. Reckoned you and Bess knew it all. "I'll get the sheep in tomorrow, Dad, I'll show you how it's done," you told me. "You and Mum can have a nice lie-in."'

It's a well-worn tale and we're laughing already. Dad carries on. 'Your mother and I are lying in bed and we hear you set off at the crack of dawn, you and Bess and the quad bike. And we all know what happened next . . .'

What happened next is family folklore. An hour later I was back, red-faced and calling the sheep all the names under the sun. They had come out the gate easily enough, but after that they had split three ways and headed off in all directions. Bess got excited and ran off after the only batch going the right way, while the rest of them opted for the wood or the main road. I had to admit defeat and came home with my tail between my legs to get help.

'I know, Dad, it was a hard lesson to learn.'

Dad nods his head and says that it only made me more determined, that I've always been as stubborn as a mule.

'And look at you now. A proper farmer, or you will be if this snow ever goes. Wait till I tell everyone at the mart.'

*　　　*　　　*

There's another heavy snowfall on New Year's Day and it will be weeks before all sign of it has gone for good. When, late in January, my moving-in day arrives, the ground is covered with a slippery slush that sits like frogspawn on top of the compacted ice. The skies have been brighter, more sunny and bluer recently, but today it is overcast and grey. There is an icy wind blowing and I wonder if there might be another blizzard on its way, but nothing is going to dampen my spirits. Tonight I will be sleeping in Fallowlees!

Mum and Dad have driven down from Hawick with a trailer to give me a hand. They set to work as soon as they arrive at Marlene Cottage, dismantling the metal runs in the back garden. I have no furniture to transport—I left it all behind with Steven when I moved out—so there are no other large items to shift apart from a single bed I've just bought from Ikea.

Dad grins when he looks at my meagre belongings sitting there waiting to go: a few suitcases of clothes, some books and photo albums, a couple of pictures.

'Lucky you travel light, eh?' he laughs. 'This isn't going to take long.'

Happily, I shut the door on Marlene Cottage

and post the keys and a card through the owners' letterbox. Fly, Roy and Alfie jump into the back of my pickup and we follow Mum and Dad through the haze.

'Hey, we're off to our new home, and you are going to *love* it.'

We take it slowly on the frozen roads, and it is a good hour before we get to the entrance to the forest. As we turn up the track, it is apparent that the forestry wagons have been back to work. The chains that allow the wheels to travel on the snow-covered surface have chewed up the road. It is peppered with water-filled craters. I watch the load on the back of Dad's pickup bouncing as he negotiates the deep ruts.

The wagons have not been as far as Fallowlees. Snow from the last snowfall, frozen into crisp particles, crunches under our wheels as we approach. It is now more than two months since Rob moved out, just before this weather hit us, and I can only be grateful that the house is so solid having stood empty all this time. I cast an admiring eye on her fortress-like two-foot-thick walls, and notice that on one side of the house there are no windows, no doubt to stop the battering from the winter storms.

I look over my fields and across the moor. The animals have gone; it makes me feel sad to see the land so empty. Something about this bleak scene reminds me of an old battlefield, of which there are many in this part of the world, and I hope it is not an omen.

Dad says he's going to have a quick look at the sheds first, as Mum and I head straight for the front door.

'Isn't it exciting,' says Mum, as we stand on the

doorstep and I take the key out of my pocket. 'I've almost forgotten what it looked like.'

'Me too. Some things are imprinted on my mind and other bits I've forgotten entirely.'

The key goes in, feels a bit awkward for a second, then turns without too much problem. The porch smells cold and damp. I open the door to the hallway and we both stand there, open-mouthed, contemplating the sight before us.

'Oh, Emma . . .!'

The corridor is awash with dirty, slushy water. Dad comes up behind us and sticks his head over our shoulders.

'Aye, there's a pipe burst in the shed as well. Suppose it's not a big surprise.'

Mum shakes her head, then gives me an encouraging prod. 'Not to worry, we'll get this cleared up in no time.'

Water must have been flowing into the house since the pipes began to thaw. Not the start I had been imagining. Mum and I get to work on the floor while Dad goes off to find the source of the leak. He soon discovers water dripping down the wall in the back room where a pipe has burst just behind the boiler. He has to rip some plasterboard off to get to it.

Mopping so much water without the right tools is a thankless task. Mum has a bucket and a towel, and all I can find is an old coal scuttle. We freeze to the bone as the water sloshes around our ankles and seeps through our jeans. My hands swell up and numb down. I try to rub some life back into them but they are just two useless lumps that don't belong to me. I can't help but remember Anna's warm, elegant handshake the last time I stood here. We begin at the front door and work our way down through the corridor into the kitchen until we are finally in the boiler room, cleaning up the last of it. By the time we're done we are all perishing and I wonder if I'll ever be able to feel my fingers and toes again.

'Wonder when we'll next see you on your hands and knees scrubbing floors,' says Dad, and we all have a laugh. I'm not the world's best cleaner.

Next on the agenda is starting up the generator, getting some electricity going. The generator has seen better days, and it refuses to oblige at first. Dad turns the key. Nothing. He turns it again and it makes a faint rumbling noise. Finally, after much persuasion, it coughs into life, pumping noxious fumes into the air and clanging like a bag of rusty hammers until it eventually settles into a steady rhythm that reminds me of an old steam train chugging away.

The big Rayburn in the kitchen won't light whatever we do. Cursing under his breath, Dad goes outside to the tank, tips it up, and that does the trick. We have heat in the kitchen at last. The rest of the house will have to wait.

It's starting to get dark. It's been a very long day and we've barely stopped to eat anything. Mum and Dad need to get back to Muirfield. They help me rig up my bed in the kitchen, give me a congratulatory hug, and head off into the night.

And now I am alone. Really alone. The dogs have been playing outside all day, occasionally trekking in dirty paw prints as they came to see what was going on. They bound up to meet me the moment I step out into the rapidly dimming light.

'This is ours,' I say to them. 'How do you like your new home?'

I look out across the fields and the moor. There

are no distant streetlights, no bobbing headlights of cars on roads, not even a hazy orange fuzz indicating another dwelling lurking in a dip. Once I have switched the generator off, the stillness that descends is almost tangible; only the scrabbling of the dogs and the cry of a bird in the trees cut through the silence.

*　　　*　　　*

I open my eyes just as it's getting light. Ooh, I'm a bit stiff from all that bending over yesterday. I stretch out and look up at the solid beams across the kitchen ceiling, thick and reassuring. I wonder again how old this place is—nobody seems to be sure. The kitchen is quite modern in other ways, with its dishwasher and fitted units. I sit up and lower my feet on to the square tiles, squealing as I do. The floor is icy cold.

Yesterday I barely had time to look at the rest of the house; now I walk through it with my cup of coffee, marvelling that this spacious, family-sized dwelling is all mine. Beyond the kitchen is the sitting room. Rob had a wood-burning stove in there, but he took that with him. The room has an open fireplace, and I picture it as it might look one day with a carpet, the fire lit and some cosy armchairs gathered round. Right now it's bare and a little forlorn looking. There's another downstairs room to the right of the entrance hall that Rob used for a dining room. Hmm, I can't see myself doing lots of entertaining, but it could be my office. Fancy, having a house with more rooms than I know what to do with! Up the steep staircase, and that bedroom with the glorious views sets my spirits soaring as soon as I walk into it.

January can be a melancholy month, but today the sun is shining again and there's a brightness in the southern sky that assails my eyes. The bathroom also faces this way and is suitably grand, though it's in a half-finished state. There's a large, free-standing bath, and work has been started to install a shower. I wonder if I could lie in the bath and look out at my kingdom through the window.

But now I've got a job to go to. Time to round up the dogs and head for Fairspring.

*   *   *

I spend a lot of time these days thinking about how I am going to make everything work out. I can't sustain a living from Fallowlees—that's been made clear right from the start—but I can make it earn its keep. My main idea is to use it as a training ground for my dogs. I have this vision of myself—one that started all those years ago with me and Bess—as a trainer of champions, winning all the competitions with my collies. The men might be able to handle all the heavier farming jobs better than I can, but there's no reason why I can't be as good a shepherd and a dog handler as the best of them. With that in mind, I decide to waste no time in bringing my five Suffolk sheep from where I have been keeping them at Fairspring, over to my farm. I probably won't be able to spend much time on them until lambing is out of the way, but I might as well get them used to their new home. I have deliberately not put them in lamb and they are very fit, bordering on fat, with nothing to do all day except feed their faces.

I borrow a trailer from Michael to bring them up one afternoon. I watch them run down the ramps and take their first, tentative steps on to the land. In no time at all they stick their heads down and start tearing at the grass in the hayfield in front of the house as if they haven't had a square meal for ages.

A Suffolk is a big, heavy-framed sheep with a strong dark brown or black face and large floppy ears. She has a deep, throaty bleat, and can even bleat with her mouth full—which is a noise that you would have to hear to believe. I myself imagine it is not far off the kind of noise you might expect to hear in some prehistoric tundra.

A Suffolk's finest attribute is her amazing growth rate; unfortunately, it is part and parcel of her worst attribute: greed. Suffolks are possibly the greediest and most selfish sheep on the planet. I have never seen an animal as focused on its stomach as a Suffolk is. I have seen portly, pregnant Suffolk ewes clear fences if there is a meal on the other side. As for the poor little lambs (who are all born jet black), spare a thought; their only mission is to keep up with Mum as she pursues her ceaseless quest for calories. She will think nothing of abandoning them if so much as a single sheep nut touches the ground two fields away. In fact, rattling a feedbag in a shed of hungry Suffolks can be a dangerous affair, as they make a deafening stampede in the direction of the food.

I cast Roy out around the field. The Suffolks are now lying contentedly in the middle of the meadow. As Roy sweeps out they spot him and get to their feet with surprising speed, making a dash for the nearest wall. To my astonishment, the leader of the group, a ninety-kilogram monster, attempts to scale it. She's not quite nimble enough and lands on top of it, knocking off the uppermost stones, then scrambles over to the other side. The other four, seeing the successful escape, follow close behind, destroying the rest of that part of the wall as they go. I watch all this helplessly from my position at the top of the field. Roy arrives at the spot where the Suffolks were lying just a few seconds earlier. He looks over at me with a puzzled expression as the rump of the last one disappears over the wall.

There's nothing we can do. They are heading straight for the thick forest, safe from bossy dogs and their even bossier owners. The forest forms an almost impenetrable cover from which it will be all but impossible to shift them.

I could scream with frustration. Who says sheep are stupid? I have worked with them all these years and they can still outfox me. I briefly consider buying some more, but there is no way I can afford it at the moment, and even if I could, it would be rare to find any that were not in lamb. I reason that no real harm can come to them, but it is a blow all the same.

The dog-training idyll will have to wait.

*   *   *

My heart always quickens when I take that left turn into the forest towards Fallowlees. I wonder when it will finally sink in that this is my farm. It certainly hasn't done so yet, three weeks after moving in. I've been out to do my supermarket shop for the month and it feels good to have that chore behind me. As I approach Redpath and am looking out admiringly at the view across my land, a sudden flash of brown skims before my eyes. I slam on the brakes but it's too late. I've hit a deer, and I seem to have hit her hard and bowled her under the pickup. I pull to a stop. In my rear view mirror I can see her thrashing wildly.

I rush back to where she is lying. Death throes, I think, as her body continues to struggle with itself. I place one hand on her head and the other on her rump to steady her and stop the violent movements. A trickle of blood runs from her nose and a large square patch of fur is missing right next to the perfect white of her tail. I wonder if I should put her out of her misery. She could be damaged internally and she might have broken some bones. I try to imagine doing it, and can't. Perhaps instead I could put her in the back of the car and take her to the vet, or even the forestry ranger.

After a few minutes, I realise that she is not about to die—at least not imminently. Her breathing is still rapid, but seems to be steadying, and the jerky spasms have stopped. I put my jacket over her head to settle her, like I have seen them do in animal rescue programmes. The last thing I want to do is leave her with a broken leg to die a painful, lingering death in the forest. I examine each limb, smoothing the brown fur. The forest is well populated with deer; I see them most nights when I walk the dogs, but I have never seen one this close to before, nor realised quite how beautiful they are. I have not found any sign of a fracture, but I have no way of assessing her further. What about internal bleeding? I help her to her feet and wait while she gathers herself. I slowly remove my jacket from her head and she stands still, if unsteadily, for a while. A minute or so later she skips off, her limbs a little uncoordinated but with an energy that surprises me. She hops into the long grass and when she thinks she is far enough away she stops and turns back to look at me, a long, slow look. I wonder if she is angry with me or grateful for my help. I watch as she bounds off into the trees.

I get back to the car, and check it for damage. Not a mark on it, just a clump of fur trapped under the number plate. For the rest of that day I think about her a lot. I hope she lives.

*   *   *

Farmers are a funny lot. I am allowed to say that. I am a farmer, the daughter and granddaughter of farmers; I have spent my entire life with farming folk; I guess I am even likely to marry a farmer. (No one else could put up with the anti-social hours I work, the lack of holidays in the sun, the muck everywhere.) They are a scruffy lot, their hands ingrained with dirt, yet most male farmers—which, the fact remains, describes most farmers—want their wives and girlfriends at their side helping with all those dirty jobs as well as to look pretty and neat and tidy. I am glad to be single at the moment and not to have to care about what anyone else thinks about me. I'm in no hurry to begin another relationship, yet I do wonder at times how I am ever likely to find a boyfriend again. I don't have many opportunities for meeting people these days, and even for a fellow farmer, Fallowlees is an isolated spot.

Archie has the same concerns. He is constantly trying to find me a husband; it has become our long-standing joke.

'I've found you a man,' he'll say. 'Got loads of money, too,' (when have I ever bothered about that?), 'and he's only fifty-five,' he will say, as an

70

afterthought.

'Archie, I've just turned twenty-four!'

'Ah well, you can't afford to be fussy out here. Never say I don't have your wellbeing at heart.'

He turns up to give me a hand at Fairspring one day and as he's leaving he tells me he's written a poem about me. I am flattered. To this day, it is one of the most thoughtful gestures anyone has ever made towards me.

'Ooh, no one's done that before,' I tease. 'What is it called, "The fool on the hill"?'

'You'll see. I'm a canny poet, me.'

I read it later when I manage to stop for a few minutes.

> As I went down by Harwood side
> A lass I chanced to see
> We talked a while, I asked her name
> Where her dwelling place might be.
>
> She said, 'My name is Emma Gray
> And I am fancy free
> With blue-grey cows and Galloway yowes
> I farm at Fallowlee.'
>
> I said, 'You are a young and bonnie lass
> It seems not right to me
> You should live your lone
> At that quiet place they call the Fallowlee
> With only blue-grey cows and Cheviot yowes
> To keep you company.'
>
> She said, 'I trust a handsome lad
> As rich as rich can be

He will come a courting out to Fallowlee
He will me wed, take me to bed
We'll have children three
With blue-grey cows and Cheviot yowes
We'll farm at Fallowlee.'

Some years have passed
Since last I went down Harwood side
I thought this day, I'll walk that way
To see if Emma yet a bride.

As I came strolling from the woods
Approaching Fallowlee
The blue-grey cows and Cheviot yowes
Were grazing peacefully.

Again I meet young Emma Gray
This tale she told to me,
'Three rich and handsome men
They all came a-courtin' out to Fallowlee.
They said we'd wed, took me to bed
Then they deserted me.
So with blue-grey cows and Cheviot yowes
I now have children three.'

At that she gave a whistle shrill and said
'Come bye to me'
Three bonny children a running came
And gathered at her knee

'Indeed,' I said, 'Young Emma Gray
You have been fancy free.'
For one was Black,
And one was white
The other was Chinese.

I chuckle as I put the piece of paper back in my pocket. Archie is not about to be appointed as the next Poet Laureate, but he can make me laugh any day.

I've just finished reading it when my friend Nikki calls my mobile. I have known Nikki for a few years now; she's a farmer's daughter too, and works as a rep for an animal minerals company.

'How's it going in the back of beyond?'

'Not you too! It's going grand. How are you?'

'Oh fine. We must catch up sometime. But listen, I met this guy who I think would be perfect for you. I thought I could set you up on a date with him.'

'You've got to be kidding!'

'It's a good idea, Em. How else are you going to meet someone? Whenever I tell anyone about you they start going on about Hannah Hauxwell. You're not turning into her, are you?'

'Well, from what I remember, Hannah Hauxwell was very contented with her life, even if it was a hard one, *and* she didn't need a man thank you very much.'

Hannah Hauxwell became a television star when she was discovered in the early Seventies living an isolated existence in the Yorkshire Dales in her family farmhouse with no electricity or running water. And no husband.

I add, 'You sound just like Archie.'

'Archie? Who's he?'

'A farmer friend. Hey, I must read you this poem he's written for me.'

'Someone's writing you poems? Well, why didn't you tell me? It doesn't sound as if you need me after all.'

'Archie's old enough to be my granddad, but he's

73

great. I suppose if you can find someone as funny as him, as good with sheep and as wise as he is, then you might be on to a winner.'

Nikki sighs. 'Emma, you can't afford to be picky. But on second thoughts, you and Crispin might not be on the same wavelength. Give me time, though. I'll find you someone.'

Chapter Five

Each night when I return home, the stark beauty of my farm startles me. Standing there on its own, with Harwood Forest to the north and west, and fields and moorland sweeping away to the south and east, it looks as if it has burst up from the ground, like a mineral part of the landscape, shaped and carved into its constituent parts by the elements over a long time. It takes me nearly fifty minutes from Fairspring to my front door, and I love the journey. I plan what I'll do first when I am back. There are so many jobs I'm just itching to get on with. My latest project is the tumbledown wall in front of the house. Bit by bit I have uncovered the large stones from the turf they have disappeared under after years and years of gradual destruction. I claw at the turf and soil to unveil each rock, but before I can rebuild it I have to demolish a bit more. It is like doing a jigsaw without a picture to follow and a bunch of broken pieces. Stone-wallers are great believers in each stone having its place in the dyke, and after persevering for hours, I can confirm this to be true—and that the space is always the last one I try! I spend hours messing around looking for suitable stones to fill in each and every gap. Bit by bit, it begins to take shape. As the holes are filled in the wall grows up once more. I'm surprised at how satisfying I'm finding this job, and can't help feeling pleased when Mum tells me on the phone one night that Winston Churchill would go out and spend time on the wall he was building whenever he needed to think or unwind.

Whenever I stop and look around me—at my farmhouse, at my land, at the view that on a clear day stretches all the way to the sea, over twenty miles away—I feel so happy and fulfilled.

One evening a few weeks later I decide that the wall looks complete. I stand back to admire my handiwork. No professional waller would be as pleased as I am—it seems to have a slight bow and to be just a bit crooked, and not all of the stones are flush; but it looks strong, and I doubt even my hurdling Suffolks could scale it to return to the flock if they ever show up again. For the thousandth time I scan the line of trees into which they disappeared. One day I thought I'd found them, but on closer investigation they turned out to be a group of mongrel sheep who must have been living wild for some time. Their fleeces were thick and seemed to contain a good selection of greenery from their adopted habitat. I wondered if I should gather them—after all, they had to belong to someone—but even as I was thinking this the leader of the pack gave the snort of alert and they bolted for the trees.

I mentioned it to a farmer down the road who verified that it was not unheard of for sheep to escape and live in Harwood Forest, grazing in the clearings and with a foolproof hiding place if they thought they were about to be caught. During the foot and mouth epidemic they would have been shot.

I retire to the house as the sun drops below the skyline. It's February and there's a cold nip in the air, the wind is blustery and biting, but it is dry. The small cluster of trees that guard the entrance to the farmhouse are skeletons of their once bushy selves. No sign of spring yet. I leave the dogs to their own devices, their kennel doors open. They all adore it here, and it feels natural for them to be able to run loose with no traffic to worry about.

The Rayburn has been a godsend. I've still got no heat in the rest of the house, but at least the kitchen is nice and warm and I've kept my bed in there, pushed up against one wall.

I wash my hands at the kitchen sink in front of the window, trying to clean the soil out from under my nails. If Nikki ever does find me a man, well, he'll have to take me as I am, I think, as I look at the dark patches at the top of each finger that never look totally clean however much I scrub them. The window looks south across my land and I can vaguely make out the form of my wall in the encroaching dark. In the garden, Alfie is trying to tempt Roy into a play fight, bowing down on his front paws and waving his tail in the air. Roy acts as if he's not bothered but as he struts past he suddenly falls on him and they wrestle in the long grass. Fly is sitting watching them both. She looks over as I turn off the tap, spots me at the window and wags her tail. When she does this her top lip lifts slightly at one side and she almost looks as if she is smiling. I have seen this before with collies; Fly's mother, Pip, could smile unlike any other dog I've come across, pulling her lips back into a full-on grin which could look quite alarming. Fly's lopsided one is more endearing. With one ear up and one down, she looks so funny; like a loveable old plonker.

The darkness is creeping closer round the house and the fields. In the short time I've been standing here the wall has almost disappeared from sight, though the dogs are lit from the porch and kitchen lights. Soon it will be pitch black, the only light coming from the moon and the stars. I busy myself

77

making something to eat. I am so alone but so very contented.

Later, I curl up all nice and warm with a cup of tea on my bed, which doubles as a sofa. My eyelids feel heavy. The lights are flickering in the kitchen, reminding me that the generator is still on. I finish my tea and force myself up and back out into the cold, settle the dogs in their kennels and am just about to walk across to the generator shed when I hear a noise beside the house. Two men are striding down the yard towards me. Oh God, they are wearing balaclavas! I freeze. Men in balaclavas . . . in the dark . . . looking very purposeful. What can they want from me? I have got no money, no expensive jewellery, no machinery. Horrors flick through my mind.

They get closer, and as they do I can see that they are wearing headlamps and carrying backpacks. Why can't I move, I think to myself, why can't I move? They are almost within reach of me now.

'Good evening,' they say as they approach. They stride on past with barely a second glance my way.

'Good evening,' I manage to croak to their backs.

It was just a couple of walkers, following St Oswald's Way—a long-distance footpath named for a seventh-century king of Northumbria, which passes through my land. It is the first time I've had an encounter like this.

My heart rate gradually settles back to normal and I even manage a slightly nervous laugh as I turn off the generator. I chatter to the dogs as I do so, and call out to them again as I make my way back to the house, as if trying to reassure myself—and anyone else who might be passing by—that I am not alone here.

A few nights later, as I'm eating dinner, I see a face peering in at my kitchen window. I scream out in shock and fear, but it turns out to be a wagon driver who has slid off the road and wants to see if I can tow him back on to the track. Apart from the odd scare like this, and losing my sheep, nothing major has happened since moving in. The only other thing that's gone wrong has been the engine of my pickup. A stone flew into it one day from the forestry track and I didn't notice the temperature gauge going up until it was too late and the engine was fried. I've had to borrow a knackered old replacement from Mum and Dad until I can afford a new engine. Heaven knows when that will be. My bank balance isn't looking very healthy.

But there's too much going on to dwell on my personal or financial worries for long. Today is scanning day at Fairspring. With Roy at my side I drive the quad bike up the steep track on the banks. The day is mizzly and cold and I can feel it penetrating my bones. I just know it is going to be one of those days when I'll never warm up properly.

It takes me a while to find the sheep. They are all grouped together, and many are sleeping.

'I know it's early, girls. I feel just the same. But there's work to do.'

They look unimpressed.

'C'mon, let's get going,' I call more loudly.

This time they rouse themselves. A few snort a warning through their noses, a reflex probably left over from days in the wild when they had to warn the others of predators approaching.

'Come bye,' I say quietly to Roy, the command

79

for a clockwise run. He has been scanning the field, waiting patiently for the command. He shoots off the bike and bolts up the hill. The sheep spot him and start to move downwards. Roy quickly runs round them, darting backwards and forwards, driving them towards me. He soon has them under his control. I always marvel at his ability as he moves the two-hundred-strong flock down through the gorse bushes and towards the pens. The sheep are fit and healthy and give him no trouble. They are safe under his authority and do not fear him so much as respect him.

I follow them all through the mist, giving Roy the odd whistle to ensure the sheep keep heading in the right direction. There are a few naughty ones: that wily old ewe with the brown face and the white muzzle is looking to escape into the farmhouse garden, while the one with the crooked ear is hoping to make a dash for that hole in the fence and out into the wood. When I first started at Fairspring, ewes like this got the better of me and Bill a lot of the time, and gathering them in would be a long, fraught affair. Gradually, through trial and error, I learnt from the sheep and from the farm itself and now I'm ready for their mischief—as is Roy. I have to second guess them all the time, anticipate what they might fancy doing rather than what I want them to do. It is known as 'sheep sense' and it can only be developed over time. Working cleverly, manipulating the flock's instincts, is a priceless knack for any shepherd to have.

The sheep are finally in the pens and, next thing I know, Davy Dick the scan man is arriving in his old jalopy.

'Hello, Davy.'

'Hello, my dear. How you doing?'

'Ah, not too bad. What about you? You full of busy?'

'Aye, flat out, you know the time of year. So how's life in the wilderness? I looked you up on Google Earth, you know. You're bloody miles from anywhere!'

I smile. 'Yeah, I know. But I really love it.'

'You're mad. A nice lass like you stuck all the way out there. It's no way to find yourself a man. Who will want to fight their way to the back of beyond to find you? You'll wind up like that Hannah Hauxwell, you know.'

'Who? Never heard of her,' I tease. 'Must be before my time.'

'You know that old woman they found living by herself on a farm in the Yorkshire Dales. Never had a man, mind. Just lived on her lonesome.'

'Really?'

'Aye, the TV cameras found her when she was old and past it. Just her, a few sheep and a few cows. She got famous after that. No one could believe a person could be living like that nowadays. And here you go looking to do the same! I heard you haven't even got any electric! How do you manage?'

He looks at me incredulously as I shrug and grin. 'She was famous, you say? Can't have been that bad, then. Be me next, maybe!'

'Hah, I doubt it. You'll be old news after Hannah. You should just find yourself a nice lad with a farm of his own and let him take care of you.'

'I had that before, but I didn't want it. I want something for myself, Davy.'

'Well, good for you. But I still think you're nuts and you'll just break your heart over that godforsaken place. It's nothing but a haven for adders and ticks.'

'Maybe you're right. But I'm going to give it a go.'

'Well, suit yourself. I'm just giving you some friendly advice. Here, come and give me a hand with this.'

'This' is Davy's scanning equipment, an odd-looking contraption consisting of a car seat positioned before a box containing the ultrasound screen. Alongside the seat—Davy's throne, and his home for most of January and February—is a crate, and as each ewe slips into the crate Davy will run a scanner over her belly. He will scrutinise the picture on the ultrasound screen, and from that he will decide whether or not she is pregnant, and if she is, how many lambs she is carrying—one, two, three, or even, very occasionally, four. He will then mark the ewe with a corresponding colour. It is the same technology they use in hospitals and Davy is very accurate at the job. I need this information so that I can feed each of my girls accordingly; there's no point in feeding a ewe who isn't even pregnant the same diet as one who is carrying triplets.

We get everything set up, and just before we start, the cavalry arrives in the form of Archie.

'Never fear, Archie's here,' says my old friend. 'Now, what do you want me to do?'

We work out a system in which Archie feeds the ewes into the long narrow race while I push each one individually into the scanning crate for Davy. I love this job, although the ewes can sometimes be unwilling and dig their hooves in at the last moment, fearful at the sight of something new. A bit of brute force usually does the trick. Watching the picture on the screen is one of the highlights of my job. When I first saw this technology, back at home in Muirfield,

I wondered how anyone could make sense of those dark and light squiggles. All I could see was what looked like chopped up cabbage and jelly beans. After a few years of watching Davy, though, I can sometimes pick out a leg or a ribcage. Occasionally, if the ewe is having only one lamb, I can make out its whole form and see its little legs waving.

It is a cold job, and there is a lot of standing around, but it gives me such a buzz. I suppose it's like having a forecast of the harvest ahead. Each life that Davy can pick out on the screen is living proof of my prowess as a shepherdess, and my job now is to make sure that bunch of squiggles on screen stays alive and becomes a healthy lamb.

The ewes are still cold and damp from the morning mist, my feet are numb and I can no longer feel the end of my nose. My hands are wrinkled and slimy from pushing the wet bodies into the crate—my gloves didn't stay dry for five minutes. It is still early, too. We have hundreds more to get through before Davy can leave.

Archie and I place bets to take our minds off our discomfort.

'I bet she's got nowt in her,' I tell Archie, pointing at an enormous white-faced mule. 'She was a proper bitch last year, could hardly keep her on the farm.'

'Nah,' says Archie. 'She'll have three.'

We watch as Davy marks her red. Twins.

'We'll call that one a draw,' says Archie.

'Emma,' says Davy suddenly. 'This one's gonna be early.'

'Really?'

'Yeah, look.'

Sure enough, the picture on the screen is larger than any of the others have been.

'She must have got out and found herself a frisky fella when I wasn't looking,' I say, looking at the two little bodies on the monitor. She will be the first to lamb. She is a dark-headed ewe with short legs. Davy marks her on the shoulder so that I'll know.

I look at the image again. 'See you two soon,' I tell them, before the ewe runs out of the crate to join the others who are already marked.

Once the first batch is all finished, I have to go to the other fields and gather in the next lot. It's a long, long morning—by the time Davy scans the last sheep we have been at it for eight hours. By now I'm desperate to know how the flock has done overall. Davy scribbles down the numbers on a bit of card and hands it over. The vast majority are carrying twins, there are eighty with triplets, around sixty singles and thirteen that aren't carrying. All in all, the flock has averaged 198 per cent, meaning that every ewe should have an average of 1.98 lambs. In reality, it rarely works like this by the time losses are taken into account, but it's a start and suddenly lambing seems very close.

After Davy has packed up and gone, Archie and I have a cup of tea and a sandwich from his old carpetbag. The hot tea warms my insides and I can forget how cold I've been for a bit. I give Michael a quick ring with the results. This is actually a nerve-racking time for a shepherd since the pregnancy rate is a direct judgement on our ability. In the past few weeks I have been scrutinising the sheep, analysing their behaviour. If one of them seems a bit too frisky, I wonder if she hasn't managed to conceive. Then I'll start wondering if I've taken good enough care of them all over the harsh winter, or if one of the tups hasn't done his job.

All these thoughts have been running through my head, but now I can put them to bed. One hundred and ninety-eight. That's a good result and Michael sounds happy, which is good since he is the one paying my wages.

As we eat, Archie cracks some jokes and asks how Alfie's training is coming on.

'Well, he's still a bit of an idiot, but he's a really good outrunner, and he's so honest as well. He always tries his best. But I'm struggling to teach him to shed. He just doesn't get it at all.'

'Well you need to make it more fun. If you get excited about it then he might too.'

'Yeah? You might be right. Maybe I've been drilling him a bit.'

'You'll have to work on it for the championship, but I reckon you'll have a good chance if you can get it right by then.'

We discuss the plans for lambing time. I tell him that Michael is bringing in a new lad, Liam, to help during the day, though I've never met him before.

'But Michael rates him highly, so we'll see. And Hilary is going to do nights.'

'Champion. And I'll be about when you need me.'

'Archie, you're a godsend.'

'Aye, well . . .'

I mean every word of it. Having somebody with his knowledge and ability makes my job so much easier. Even just his company can help to break up a long day.

Archie thrusts the plastic ice-cream box towards me. 'Have a scone.'

'Honestly, I'm all right, Archie, thanks.'

He shakes his head. 'No, you take one. Eileen made them. You need fattening up. No use if you're all bones. You need some homely curves; that's what men like 'n'all. Something to grab hold of.'

'Oh, OK,' I say giggling. I'm not sure if Archie's idea of feminine beauty is the same as mine but I don't need to count the calories in this job—which is just as well, since the scone comes generously layered with butter and homemade bramble jam.

Now it's time to gather up all the sheep Davy has marked. Archie runs them up the narrow race while I stand next to the shedder gate, shedding them into their different groups: barren ewes, single ewes, twins and triplets.

Now we just have to count down till lambing. This is when the hard work for a shepherd really begins. From now on the sheep will need a lot of attention as the lambs inside them reach maturity. Their daily feed will consist of concentrates as well as the haylage they have been getting since the snow. Any hopes of a social life for me will have to be put on hold until the end of April at the earliest. The ewes have to come first.

*   *   *

Roy has worked so hard today. I'm pleased with him and he knows it, but being Roy he's cool as anything, just accepts the praise as if it's his due and shrugs it off. Now he's snoozing in the back of the pickup as we travel home together.

I bought Roy from Paul Bristow, who was the shepherd at Kirkley Hall when I was studying there for my advanced national certificate in sheep management. We students would often help him on the farm, and I got to see his young dog, Bill, grow and develop into a first-class work dog. Bill had an easy way about him and commanded respect from both sheep and cattle. After I left college I followed his progress through the farming papers and saw how well he did in the nursery trials held over the winter. All went quiet after that as Paul was too busy with other work to compete in the summer.

One day out of the blue I got a phone call from Paul saying that he had a couple of pups left from a litter by Bill. They were four months old now, so I guessed he had been struggling to sell them. He told me I was more than welcome to come and see them for myself, and I was more than happy to take him up on the offer.

There were two pups, one perfectly marked with a big white rough collar and four white paws, the main part of his body a sleek and shiny black. The other was black all over barring a small snip of white on the end of his nose and a little splash of white on his chest. He was still growing and clearly going through the gangly stage, his adult coat just coming in. He looked a bit scruffy compared to his sibling.

Paul suggested we take them out and watch them play round the yard and steading. They were just typical pups cavorting about, with nothing much to differentiate one from the other. Neither showed much interest in me or Paul; they were quite happy sniffing about and gadding around with each other. I had almost decided on the nicely marked pup that was the spit of his father, which couldn't be a bad thing. The other one looked more like his mother who, although a nice dog, was a complete handful when it came to sheep and had been known to bring them down in a rather lupine way.

'Shall we see what they make of the sheep?' said Paul.

Four months is young to train a collie, but it is always interesting to see if they show an aptitude early on. We stepped through the gate into a field of pedigree Suffolks. Paul shook a feedbag and they came galloping over to us. The pups didn't notice what we were up to until the sheep were virtually at our feet. Then they pricked up their ears and came into the field. The one with the nice markings bounced around the flock yapping madly, his tail wagging with excitement. The black one was different; when he got close to the sheep his head went down, like a lion stalking his prey. He then cast out right round this little group.

I looked across at Paul. He, too, was watching this little scrap of a pup with an expression that suggested he couldn't quite believe what he was seeing. The dog kept running until, at the perfect point of balance—twelve o'clock to our six o'clock—he stopped and walked directly towards the surly bunch. That was it, I'd seen enough.

'I'll take that black one,' I said to Paul.

'I thought you might.' He grinned ruefully. 'He's never done that before, you know, or I'd have kept him. But I know he'll have a good home with you.'

We went inside to draw up his certificate. That was how I bought Roy, the best one hundred and fifty pounds I have ever spent. And how he's flourished from that gangly youth to the thick-coated, shiny black dog he is today!

Chapter Six

One of the first things I did once I had settled in to Fallowlees was go home to pick up Bill. I had missed him terribly. Luckily he is an adaptable old stick, and it took him no time at all to make himself at home and get stuck in to his favourite pastime: hunting for moles. Happily for him, Fallowlees is a moley paradise.

Moles have long been a fascination of Bill's, and he can often be found staring longingly at a molehill. If I ask him, 'Hey, Bill, where are the moles?' he will start digging at the heaps of soil with gusto, and many is the time I have found a crater of his making and Bill nearby, his whole face covered—nose black and impacted with earth, mouth full of the stuff as well, trapped between his gums and teeth. Sometimes he yelps with excitement or barks with frustration, while Fly eggs him on, *yipp-yipp*, like a cheerleader in the background. If I pop my head round the corner to see what all the fuss is about, Bill will run between me and the crater, eager to show me what a good boy he has been hunting down those pesky creatures. And yet, in all the years we've been together, I've never actually seen Bill catch one.

The ground in front of the house and garden is strewn with molehills. The moles pose a problem that, with no one besides me bothered about solving it— and nothing but local predators to keep them under control—is getting worse. The mole population is multiplying at an alarming rate. In desperation, I decide I need to call in the professionals.

The mole man arrives armed with a selection of

devices which work like mousetraps—they are spring-loaded and triggered when a mole passes through. For a second I feel a bit guilty as I've always held a 'live and let live' sort of attitude. But I tell myself not to be daft. I can't let this get out of hand.

The first thing the mole man does is wash his hands with soil so that when the moles come upon the trap—relying heavily on their sense of smell—there is nothing to arouse their suspicion. He works out which way the tunnels run and marks each trap with a bamboo stick so that he will be able to check them when he returns.

A few days later I am pottering around in the kitchen preparing breakfast. I make a cup of tea and put my porridge in the microwave. While it's heating I pad over the cold tiles in my bare feet to the porch where Bill has his basket. No frost today, I think, as I look into the garden, but the wind is shaking the trees and I bet it's chilly out there.

Then I see it, and scream.

Slap bang in the middle of the porch, completely enclosed within one of the traps, is a fat, swollen, ghoulish and very, very dead mole . . . And sitting in his basket, looking extremely pleased with himself, is Bill, coated from nose to tail in soil.

'Oh, Bill, honestly!' I say in reprimand, putting on my sternest face. Bill drops his gaze to his feet as if to say, 'But I couldn't help it!'

I can't bear this doleful expression of his and I soften in seconds. He sneaks a look at me out of the corner of his eye and seeing me smiling he looks up and wags his tail, then looks towards the trap and back at me.

'You are *such* a messy old clown, Bill.'

He barks, jumps up and puts his paw over his prize;

and that, dear friends, is the story of the first mole, Bill ever caught.

*   *   *

Despite the fact that Fly and Roy are my main trial dogs, Alfie has fast been moving up the ranks. For a long time I doubted he had the brains to make it in competition, but over the winter he has come on in leaps and bounds such that, despite the snow putting paid to some of the nursery trials, I've managed to compete with him in four of them. To my delight, Alfie has picked up second prize in one of them, meaning that he qualifies for the Northumberland championship at the end of the season.

Nursery trials are held in the winter months and are specifically for dogs that are less than three years old at the end of that calendar year. Their main purpose is to give young dogs some experience without having to face competition from more practised trial dogs. Originally they were seen as more of a training aid, but now they are becoming more and more competitive, and the standard seems to rise year on year.

Most trials follow a similar pattern. The handler stands at the post, dog by his or her side. At their command, the dog sets off on what is called the 'outrun', making a wide circle around sheep that may be over four hundred yards away. The dog approaches the sheep and starts to move them towards its handler in a procedure known as 'the lift'. This is followed by 'the fetch', in which the dog brings the sheep in a controlled manner through a set of gates towards the handler, taking the sheep close-to and behind the handler ready to start the next phase, known as 'the drive'. The drive usually takes place over a triangular course, and the dog must take the sheep through two more sets of gates in as straight a line as possible, and sometimes with obstacles in the way in order to emulate real working conditions. The next part can vary according to the competition, but the dog must also demonstrate its ability to 'shed' the sheep—to separate one or two from the others—and to 'pen' them. The handler is permitted to leave the post for this part of the operation.

Points are not awarded for good behaviour and practice as such, but are deducted for any errors or for over-assistance from the handler, and misdemeanours such as biting a sheep would lead to instant disqualification.

Championship day arrives and I wake up early and excited. I let the dogs out for a run, and watch their steamy breath leave trails in the freezing cold morning air. The trial is held on the coast and the roads are icy on the drive over there. It feels even colder at our destination, but at least it is bright and clear. There are already a good few people waiting to take part when I arrive, every one of them looking like they have done this before. People have wrapped themselves up in layer upon layer of outdoor kit; they mean business, dressed to last the duration, intent on maximum heat storage.

All the qualifying handlers draw a number out of the hat to decide the running order. I will run last, the upside of which is that I can gauge how the sheep are behaving, the downside of which is that it gives me plenty of time to get nervous.

I watch the other handlers. The sheep are capricious. They lull you into a false sense of security as they walk quietly round most of the course, as meek as can be, then respond to just a bit too much pressure by galloping off unexpectedly, or dodging the gates, both of which are instant points losers.

My turn comes and, as anticipated, I am terribly nervous. I walk up to the post with Alfie at my side. With the possible exception of Fallowlees on a bad day, I think that post must be the loneliest place in the world. Alfie has seen the sheep at the top of the field and he is ready for the off. He stands a few feet away from me, his eyes locked on to the four woolly creatures three hundred yards away. I call *'Away!'*, my command for Alfie to take an anti-clockwise route towards them, and he shoots off like a rocket. I can hear his feet thundering, eating up the frozen ground. As he comes to the top of his outrun, he slows naturally as I have taught him to do to avoid spooking the sheep. A blast of the whistle and he stops, bang on. My heart starts to pump harder. A good lift is the secret to a good trial. Liken it to being introduced to someone for the first time—if that person is rude to you from the outset, you are less likely to respond well than you would if they were polite. Alfie calmly and quietly walks towards the sheep and, sensing that he means business, they begin to move in a direct line towards me. Yes! I'm on my way. The rest of the course passes in what seems no time at all, the sheep moving at a gentle trot, hitting both sets of hurdles right through the middle then entering the pen with just a little persuasion.

Last of all comes the shed—Alfie's weak point. We must work together on this. We have spent many hours practising to split batches of sheep but he is just not a natural shedder like Roy is. I take a deep breath and hope that his excellent work so far will not all fall apart in the home stretch. We move together to sandwich the sheep between us and suddenly—whether by good luck or good management I will never know—a gap appears in the fold. I call Alfie, who bolts in and splits the chosen sheep off.

'OK!' shouts the judge to signify that the shed is acceptable. The trial is over. I take the sheep to the exhaust pen at the bottom of the field, practically skipping with joy. I just know that my run was better than any of the others; but judging is a subjective matter and I can't really predict how it will go.

We must look an odd bunch as we huddle round the judge's car waiting for the results. We spend all week out in the cold and rain with our dogs and a load of sheep for company, and how do we choose to spend our free time—shopping, a movie, lolling around in bed listening to Metro Radio, stuffing ourselves with ice-cream and shortbread? No. We choose to get up at cockcrow and head out with the dogs and a load of sheep all over again. It would be hard to explain to most people.

There is no *X Factor*-style build up to the results. We don't even get them in reverse order. Paul, chairman of the Northumberland Sheepdog Trials League, simply announces the winner: me!

I go up to collect my trophy. I try to stay measured and modest, but inside I'm as happy as Larry. Alfie and I are the nursery champions!

The other competitors come forward to congratulate me, and a group of us head to the pub to celebrate.

*   *   *

Back at Fallowlees the sky is dazzling. There are so

many stars, they seem to be touching each other. The moon is shining so brightly, almost as bright as day. The grass is glistening with a gemstone frost that makes a crunch-crunch-crunch as Alfie and I fetch the other dogs for our last walk of the day, up behind the farmhouse towards the small lake. We are the only movement. When I reach the top of the hill I turn and look down at my home, a fairytale cottage, moonlit and spell-cast. I stay gazing at it like a mother admiring her sleeping infant. I know I should call the dogs, but I don't want to spoil the silence. Not just yet.

Back at home, I put the dogs to bed before heading off to mine. I have finally moved from the kitchen up to the bedroom. Even though it is still very chilly upstairs, I was desperate to wake up to that brilliant view in the mornings; I haven't even bothered to buy curtains. Even with all the clear-skied light flooding in unchallenged, I slip quickly into a deep and peaceful sleep.

*   *   *

I may not be bothered about curtains, but carpet under my feet on a cold morning is imperative so a few days before the trial I had decided to take a trip over to Newcastle to buy one. The busy city centre is always a shock to the system. Not just the sheer volume of shoppers, but also the way it is such a regular part of life for most people. The jostling throng, the rushing around, the busy roads with vehicles hurtling past at perilous proximity—for me it is sensory overload. I am anxious about spending money, anxious about being lost in the crowd, anxious about annoying people, anxious about how

95

I look, anxious about being anxious . . . All this for a boring old carpet.

I deliberately tried to avoid looking at shop windows on the way to the carpet store. No point in getting diverted by fashionable clothes I could not afford and would not wear. I had come for a carpet, and I would leave with a carpet—it sounded easy enough until I saw the bewildering range of rugs on offer. Roll upon dizzying roll of them. All I wanted was a cheap way to save my bare footsies from the shock of bare floorboards, but that seemed about as easy as finding a needle in a haystack. All I could see was an ugly brown carpet with a mesmerising swirly design and a no less mesmerisingly hefty price tag. A salesman was making a beeline in my direction and I had to scamper off to the bargain basement (I have an instinctive dislike of sales patter). When I emerged half an hour later, I felt unaccountably proud of myself: I had a carpet, free fitting and delivery, and as I left the metropolis behind, I thought about my achievements since striking out on my own, and how something as prosaic as buying a carpet can be just as important as the more romantic milestones, like a first house or (as I would learn a few days later) winning first prize.

*   *   *

Mum and Dad are going to need their pickup back soon and I still can't afford a new engine for mine. Feeling hopeful, I make my way to Hexham machinery sale—or the Hexham scrap sale as some call it—where the farmers from around these parts bring all the oddments they no longer have any use for to sell or trade. You never quite know what you might find there—I've seen everything from henhouses to tractors, old lampposts to horse carts. Each lot tells a story of a useful life. For most, the story ends here, sold for scrap; but for others the sale opens a new chapter, as they will be reused.

Today there are a few cars, but most are ancient or have far too many miles on their clocks. However, cars at this sale are notoriously cheap—even if it is usually for a reason. I hang around all day waiting for the cars to be sold. The first, a diesel, goes for five hundred pounds, which is way over my budget. The next goes for two thousand, then nine hundred, then three-fifty—still too dear. The penultimate car to go under the hammer is a bright yellow Hyundai Accent. I have my bidding finger ready. The auctioneer starts at three hundred pounds. He looks around but there are no bids, so he drops to one hundred. I raise my finger. He goes up in twenties. By the time I have bid one-eighty I am looking round anxiously, not wanting to seem desperate. One of the other bidders shakes his head. A few more seconds and the hammer falls and I am the owner of a clapped-out bananamobile!

I have no idea if it will even start. It is amazingly cheap for a car, but bloody expensive if it doesn't take me anywhere! Writing up a cheque for that amount hurts considerably with my finances the state they're in. I get a closer look at it and can't help thinking how unsuitable it is: low to the ground for a start, which is hardly ideal for the forestry track, and it has painted black alloy wheels and a spoiler, suggesting that it used to belong to a boy racer, a motor head. No 'careful lady owner' here! But I could not care less about its appearance if it gets me from A to B safely. It is going to be full of dogs anyway. I imagine the previous owner, all swagger and baggy jeans, watching in horror as a girl drives past in his old car, wellies in the passenger seat, collie dogs in the back, and laugh out loud.

I unlock the door and find that it has central locking, something I've never had before. It looks immaculate inside. I sit in the driver's seat and look at all the controls. It has also got electric windows and a sunroof. I am aware that some of the people who watched me buy it are now standing around, pretending not to be interested, but dying to find out if I've got a bargain or a dud. I bet they would love it if it didn't start and I pray I won't give them that satisfaction. I pretend to fiddle around in the glove box until the crowd dissipates a little and then I slide the key into the ignition and turn. The engine coughs a few times and then hums into life, first time. Yes! I look up to see people still watching. Right, now to see if it drives. I let out the clutch and off we go, out of the mart and on our way. I have a new set of wheels! How long it will last is anyone's guess—it pulls to the left when mobile, and to the right when I brake; there is a hole in the exhaust; and who knows if her sump will hold out on the forestry track, if there will be punctures galore—but these are minor worries if she'll serve her purpose. For the time being I'm back on the road.

*   *   *

Banana car is not the only new addition to the family. I had been looking to increase my pack of dogs, and Fallowlees gave me ample space to do so. I had hoped that Fly would come into season soon and I could line her to Bill, Roy's father, but she is showing no signs. When I heard that three pups were available from a litter resulting from a mating of Roy's mother and father, I was pretty excited, and crossed my fingers for a nice little bitch like Fly.

It was a disappointment to discover they were all boys. Two were jet black, just like Roy, and the third was a little tricolour. The black pair jumped all over me, keen to show what little stars they were. The other one didn't seem interested, and just sat in the kennel while the others cavorted about. I don't know why but I liked him from the start. He looked like a thinker, and despite the fact I had always been told to pick the boldest pup in a litter, I felt something for this little fellow. I picked him up and named him there and then. Len, after Grandpa—the same grandfather who gave me my first dog, and who worked the family farm with my uncle right up until his death a few years ago.

'Better be a good one,' I told the little scrap. 'Better do the name justice.'

I bonded with Len straight away. He isn't independent like Roy or hero-worshipping like Alfie. In fact, he's more like Fly. He likes to be near me, and without any training walks perfectly to heel, so close he almost touches my legs. He has deep, dark brown eyes that will melt a fair few hearts.

He makes me laugh, too. One evening in the kitchen he spots a beetle and rushes over to it. Then he bows down on his front legs, his head flat to the floor, watching it intently as the beetle continues its trek across the tiles. Len runs around it and lets out a high-pitched squeak. He lays a paw on it gently then quickly lifts it off, barks once, then does a mad circuit of the kitchen before going back to watching it again. From her place on the sofa, Fly barely deigns to acknowledge him. I can almost see her thinking to herself, '*Youngsters*,' and letting out an exasperated sigh.

Just as I hope, Len proves a natural talent and easy to train.

Although he's still young, I decide to give him his first introduction to the sheep at Fairspring and take him out with a long washing line attached to his collar in case he is unruly. I have also put a muzzle on him, which he objects to massively, rubbing his face along the ground as he tries to free himself of the contraption. The muzzle is a necessary evil when I do not know what his first reaction will be—dogs are wolves after all, and the wolf's instinct is to bring down its prey. The welfare of the flock has to take priority at all times.

Anything can happen when you take a dog to sheep for the first time. Usually the young pup will be so excited that he will rush straight in and cause havoc. Some will try to bite the sheep and to split one off from the rest of the flock, isolate it and wear it down like a wild animal would do. Occasionally a youngster will stalk them like a lion stalking a gazelle in the wild. And, very occasionally, it will show no interest at all.

I am hoping that Len will not be in the latter category, especially with his breeding. He has such a biddable nature and I have high hopes for him. I get Alfie to gather the sheep in the middle of the field and watch Len's reaction. He stops thinking about the muzzle and stares intently. A good start.

I let out the line and Len shoots off, flying straight through the middle of the small flock, scattering them in all directions. I quickly whistle at Alfie to gather the fragmented party together, and while Len gathers himself after his little outburst, I walk over to him.

'Hey, you,' I growl. 'No!'

Len, always so willing to please, has never heard me shout at him before. He looks startled. Instead of launching a repeated dash at the flock, he stands for a second and seems to think first about what he could have done wrong. I can almost see the cogs whirring. Then his head goes down and he walks over to the re-gathered flock, at a steady pace, right behind them, bringing them over to me.

'Good lad, good lad,' I croon. I move around and he moves too to keep the sheep coming in my direction. This is natural balance at its best. It is as if we are all on a clock face, with me at six o'clock and Len at twelve, and every time I move, Len mirrors me to ensure we hold our equal opposition with the sheep between us and right by my feet.

The sheep have settled and are moving happily away from Len as he crosses from side to side, constantly echoing my movements.

'Good lad,' I keep on telling him.

Every so often he gets excited and runs in and splits one off, but it is to be expected in a young enthusiastic dog and this is why I have the long line on him.

I made a good choice.

*   *   *

Mum and Dad are coming to fetch the pickup this weekend, so I set off for a last look for the missing Suffolks while I still have the chance. I sometimes go out in the evening just as the sun is setting, figuring that's the time they're most likely to appear. I drive along the rutted road that leads to the lake. Tiny trees fight for existence along the verges. Heather is abundant but not yet in bloom.

The lake water is smooth in the grassy glade. It's pretty wild up here, with only the deer to nibble on the grass. Once upon a time this area would have been part of the farm, but it has long since been taken over by the encroaching of the fir trees. I travel on past the nearly derelict house that was once a neighbouring farm but is now abandoned, like Redpath. It sits amid a huge garden of rhododendrons—what a picture it is going to make when they are in flower.

As I drive I'm scanning the trees and the clearings for any sign of my woolly monsters. I am a bit more worried about their health now I know that adders like the mix of habitats round here, and ticks are another problem.

On a hill some distance away, I spot moving shapes. Yes, I'm sure it's my little flock this time, clambering in amongst recently felled trees, grazing together and looking more like mountain goats than prizewinning domestic sheep. They are a long way off and there is no road in that direction but something has been this way before and left a barely distinguishable track. I wonder if I can sneak up on them. Fly, Roy and Alfie have been running alongside and I call for them to get in the car with me. Alfie and Roy hop into the back while Fly jumps in the front to join Bill, who always likes to travel in the passenger seat to watch what is going on.

The proto-track is wet, and even in four-wheel drive the pickup is slipping and clearly not up to it. There's no option but to get out and try to capture them on foot.

'Roy,' I whisper, and he jumps down. The pair of us head quickly and as quietly as we can up the steep slope. It's not easy as the ground is littered with branches and large stumps. The sheep are feeding, still oblivious to our presence. When we are about one hundred and fifty yards away, they seem to sense something. Their heads jerk upwards like hunted gazelles and their bodies tense. But Roy will be able to outfoot them easily.

'Away,' I say, and he shoots off like a rocket, but the Suffolks are not ready to give up their freedom just yet. By the time Roy gets close they have reached the cover of the trees. I send him in after them with an optimistic whistle, but I know it is hopeless. It is dark and hard to move in there. Sure enough, ten minutes later Roy emerges empty handed, looking a bit guilty.

'It's OK, Roy, it's not your fault.' But he always brings the sheep back and he's upset that he might have done something wrong.

Well, at least they are fit, I think in consolation as I pick my way back down to the car.

Chapter Seven

Lambing arrives and I have a vicious cold. Every inch of me aches, my nose is running and my throat is so sore that my ears hurt. Not the way you want to feel when you have to be up at five a.m. to work flat out, often without a break, until at least six p.m.

It is a frosty morning and the wind bites deep into me, right through my layers. I blow my nose and set off for the fields on the quad bike. I've got Fly, Roy and Alfie with me and they run alongside the bike, never in front. It helps to keep them fit.

I've attached the snacker to the quad—a metal trailer which puts out a one-kilo drop of feed at even intervals. At each field I give a shout, 'C'mon, girls!' and my ewes come running from wherever they happen to be, their girths so extended now that they look comical as they bumble over for their breakfast. The dogs keep the sheep from getting too close to the bike and the snacker and prevent the over-eager ones from getting in between the two and being run over—something that has been known to happen. Though it rarely does any damage, I am careful to avoid it. The sheep look healthy and happy. Their lambs are due in a few days' time but I'm keeping them outside until the very last moment because it is more natural for them to be in the open air and their fleece is adequate protection against the harsh weather. Lying around in the sheds for too long beforehand can cause birthing difficulties.

My rounds have revealed nothing untoward, until, in the last field, I see straight away that one ewe is standing by herself. Sheep are flock animals and it is rare that an individual will separate from the others unless there is something wrong with her.

I feed the rest of the flock then go to investigate. She is standing next to a hay feed, guarding two perfect Texel lambs. As she sees the dogs approaching she stamps one of her front feet on the ground as a threat. I order the dogs to stay on the bike and park a little distance away.

As I get close I can see the lambs are dry, full of milk and seem contented. The mother has a dark face and is in good condition. I can tell by the notch in her ear that she is three years old and will have had lambs the previous year. Satisfied that the little family is well, I leave them alone, but decide that now is the time to bring the rest of the flock inside. I have already spent days bedding the four sheds in the steading with straw, making sure there is hay and that the water troughs are clean, and I have built small, individual pens so that as each sheep lambs she can bond with her newborns in more intimate surroundings.

While my hands are free I blow my nose again, wishing I was at home in bed, then I set out with Fly to gather in the flock. I choose Fly because she is the least pushy of my dogs and won't be rough with the ewes as they are obviously more vulnerable than usual. She fires round the field at high speed until she reaches the top. A whistle drops her like a bullet, and another softer, lower whistle sets her on her way, carefully walking the sheep down the field towards the sheds. The expectant mothers are in no state to try to oppose her, and they allow themselves to be ushered towards their new quarters. Fly works quietly and gently, as I knew she would.

Getting all of the sheep into the sheds takes most

of the day and the light is fading as I shut the door on the last batch. I look over them before I leave. Some are pulling at the hay, but most are lying contentedly chewing their cuds—the calm before the storm. The next few weeks will be manic. After checking the new family out in the field, I head for Fallowlees and an early night.

*   *   *

I was curious to meet Liam, the new recruit. I had heard a lot about him from Michael who really rated him, said he was enthusiastic and resourceful and could use his initiative. He had proved himself a capable tractor driver over the summer harvest on Michael's own farm, and now Michael had enlisted him to help me on the day shift while we were lambing. I have to admit I was dubious. It is rare to find a tractor driver who is any use with sheep. Unlike machines, sheep are unpredictable and frustrating at the best of times. Tractor drivers find it difficult to fathom a sheep's mind (perhaps, it has occurred to me, because they are mainly men and the sheep are mainly women!).

Liam rocks up fifteen minutes late, which doesn't put me in the best of moods, especially as I've turned up twenty minutes early thinking he might be early, too, for his first day.

'Alreet?'

He climbs off his motorbike. He's tall and attractive with a muscular build, dark hair swept up in an Elvis Presley quiff. Mmm, quite fanciable and not quite what I was expecting. But he's also young, which comes as a surprise. He can't be more than eighteen. I feel awkward. I want to get things straight right from the start, to let him know that it won't be acceptable if he turns up at this time again, but confronted with this smiling young man, I back off slightly.

'Right, we need to get going straight away.' I look at my watch in an obvious manner. 'I'll show you what you're going to need to do. And I have to warn you, things are going to get very busy, very soon.'

God, I sound like a right battle-axe. This is silly. It would be far better to make friends with him than to start laying down the law. As I show him round the steading, pointing out where everything is, giving him an idea of some of the jobs we'll soon find ourselves doing, I become more relaxed.

'So, what do you know about sheep?' I ask him with a smile.

'Well,' he begins, 'me mate lives on a farm so I help out there, like, ya kna, when it's busy, with shearin' and stuff.'

'Oh, that's good.' It sounds as if he might have actually gleaned a little sheep sense in the process, which is a relief. If he hasn't, he's going to be little good to me.

'And lambing, too?'

'Neh, none of that.'

'Oh.' That's a blow. Still, he must have picked something up. 'I hear you like driving tractors.'

'Oh aye. I quite fancy a farm of me own, just like Michael's, lots of fields, like, and great big machines.'

'And sheep?' I offer hopefully.

He glances quickly across at me, then looks away. 'Oh aye, I quite like sheep 'n' all.'

'Good. That'll help just a bit for the next few weeks.'

We agree that Liam will help me from eight in the morning until around five in the afternoon, but that he'll stay for longer if I need him. He will help me feed the ewes in the morning and at night, take the newly delivered ewes and their lambs out during the day and make sure that all of them are well bedded with straw.

By the time we've finished the grand tour, I may still be doubtful about his desire to work with sheep, but I'm confident that we're going to get on grand. We natter about the nightlife in Hexham and the nightclub Dontinos, and despite the fact I'm a few years older, I find that we know some of the same people. Liam fills me in on all the gossip I've missed over the last couple of months.

'You don't get out much, do you?' he says incredulously.

*　　　*　　　*

Day three of lambing and Liam is shouting something at me from the yard. I can't hear him so I come out of the pen where I've just finished milking a ewe and make my way towards him.

'There's a dead ewe in the far shed,' he says.

'What?'

'She's dead.'

'I was just in there five minutes ago and they were all fine.'

'Well, she's a goner now.' He shrugs his shoulders.

I sigh and follow him across the yard. We go into the far shed and, sure enough, there she is stretched out on her chest, her back legs stuck out behind her. She is completely limp and her head is lolling to the side, her eyes are glazed and her jaw is slack. A little dribble of saliva trails out of the corner of her mouth.

'See,' says Liam. 'Told ya.'

I prod her and get no response. I roll her on to her

side and get a closer look. I tap the sensitive bit of skin just in front of her eye and her lids react ever so slightly. She is alive, but only just.

Milk fever. Calcium deficiency. She has all the characteristics, but it might just be too late and I switch into emergency mode. First I run and grab the bottle of medicine, Calciject, that she needs to receive. Then I pull out a ten-millilitre syringe and a sharp needle, draw in the clear fluid, lean heavily on the ewe so that the large milk vein that pumps blood from her heart to her udder becomes more prominent, slide the needle in and draw it back. A rush of blood flows into the syringe. Bingo. I slowly start to depress the plunger, shooting medicine directly into the vein. About halfway through the process, still leaning on the ewe, I feel her muscles tighten.

'Hold her,' I tell Liam.

By the time the syringe is empty, she is starting to thrash and fight to be free of us. I let her stand up and she waddles a short distance away and starts to sneeze and cough. Fluid has been building in her lungs while she was unconscious, so this is to be expected. She waddles a bit further and has a wee (always a good sign). She is heavy in lamb and the stress of her progressing pregnancy combined with the filling of her rather substantial udder has been too much. The injection provided her with a vital hit of calcium. Had we been any later in attending to her, she would not have survived. The condition can be hard to spot until the final stages since ewes in late pregnancy often appear lethargic and lazy. Thankfully Liam was quick off the mark and this ewe and her two unborn lambs will live to fight another day.

Liam looks at me in surprise—admiration, perhaps—and we both stand there watching her. I'm feeling rather pleased with myself, too. It is rare that saving an animal is quite so spectacular, so immediately rewarding.

'We'll catch her after she's fully recovered and inject her with some more calcium under the skin. It's slower releasing and will give her a steady supply. And we'll mark her with a big red C so we can keep an eye on her.'

Liam seems lost for words. I laugh. 'You OK?'

'Aye, I think so. Can I do that next time?'

'Of course you can.'

Liam will be on the lookout for ewes with calcium deficiency from now on. If he ever comes across a dead ewe—not uncommon at lambing time—he will be found touching its eye in search of that flicker of life, just in case.

*   *   *

It's still dark, though there's a patch of light in the east that suggests that morning is on its way. I pull up to the shed. The pickup's gone, so it's just me and the banana now. It has only just started to warm up—there is still some ice on the corners of the windscreen—and I'm reluctant to get out. My sore throat is better but I have a tickly cough now instead, and I'm still miserably snivelling. I open the door and get out, my breath freezing in front of me as I walk across the yard. The lights are on in the lambing sheds and I wonder which one Hilary is in. I see that the sheep in the long shed have been disturbed so I guess she's in there.

I have to weave my way through the sheep to reach

110

her. Some of them are so heavy and so used to people walking amongst them now that they make no effort to move out of the way and I have to step over them.

Hilary looks tired and has a faint purple hue under her eyes. That's what twelve hours' non-stop lambing does to you.

'Hey, was it a busy night?'

'Not too bad. About thirty. How's the cold?'

'Getting better slowly, thanks. I'll try not to breathe on you.'

We walk past the individual pens, and Hilary gives me the case notes on each newly lambed ewe. I often think the lambing shed is a bit like a maternity ward and we are nurses. Each mum has an enclosed area to bond with her offspring, and she will be waited on hand and foot while she is there. If she has a medical problem, or a weak lamb, she might stay in a pen of her own for longer. We check the pens regularly, delivering fresh food and water, making sure all our patients are fit and well. We lift up the lambs to check that their little tummies are full of colostrum, the essential, nourishing first milk that ewes produce.

Hilary updates me on who has been born during the night and on the bed blockers who have been in for a few days. There are only eighty individual pens, so it is essential to keep the ewes moving, some heading out as others come in.

The ewe we are looking at now gave birth three days ago while she was feeding at the trough. 'Talk about multi-tasking,' said Hilary. 'Mum sneezes and this pair shoot out.' Her offspring are a pathetic sight. They are Charolais sheep, with very little woolliness on their bones. They have inherited their father's characteristics. Their spindly little legs are almost smooth, as are their heads; they look strangely wizened and aged.

We lean on the gate. 'I reckon these two could go out today, don't you think, Hilary?'

She agrees. 'They're full as guns and she's got loads of milk.'

'Mmm. Shame she's such a rubbish mother, though.'

The ewe is a three-year-old Mule—a cross-breed, my favourite. This is her second pregnancy. Mules usually make exceptional mothers, but judging by the attitude of this one, I wonder if her previous lambs survived. She is busy stuffing her face, and although she lets her young suckle her, she shows little interest in their welfare. Yet they have improved considerably since their birth and although their lack of wool makes them look totally weedy, they are energetic and should manage to keep up with her.

I make my mind up. 'Yep, I'll get them out this morning.'

The ewe in the next pen provides a stark contrast. She gave birth only hours ago but mutters constantly at her lambs, nudging them towards her teats. She stamps her foot at us threateningly as we watch her, nodding her head, daring us to come closer.

'Well, *they* won't be in there long,' I say.

Lambs born to mothers like this are fortunate, and they have a much greater chance of survival.

We repeat the procedure in the other sheds. Very few of the individual pens are empty, and even while we are doing our rounds I see ewes starting to show signs of labour. Well, we can hardly expect them to wait for a suitable moment. I say goodnight to Hilary, and she gladly goes home to her bed. I watch her disappear feeling so jealous I could weep; I could quite easily go back to bed myself.

Something catches the corner of my eye in the yard and I groan: Houdini. Again. Every day I have to round her up and put her back inside. I go to the car and let Roy out. One word, and he knows his job. He shoots round the delinquent creature and herds her towards the door of the shed I've just opened. This time I am putting her in with the ewes that are expecting three lambs. I figure that the extra rations might be enough to keep her from straying, or even just weigh her down a little and tame her frisky nature.

'You're my little escape artist,' I say to her. I watch with an exasperated smile as she makes her way over to the rack of hay, pulling at it in hungry clumps. She isn't a large sheep, in fact she's not very well developed at all. I wonder if she was a pet lamb, which would account for her bad behaviour and smaller stature (pet lambs often don't grow as well as those reared naturally).

'You stay there this time, you hear me.' She ignores me, and carries on munching her breakfast.

I begin my routine on autopilot. I let the dogs out to run around and please themselves while I check the sheds. When I am satisfied that all is well, I begin to ring and mark the lambs I deem ready to face the outside world today. The sun has broken through now and its warmth makes me feel better; a nice mug of steaming coffee would help even more but this job has to come first. I start with the bad mother. I climb into her pen and lift up each lamb, checking that their stomachs are full and that they appear to be healthy. Hilary is right; they each have a tankful. I stretch a small orange rubber ring over a metal instrument that allows me to transfer it on to the lambs' tails. Lambs are born with enormous tails, almost to the ground, but they have an infant's amazing capacity to shit all over them. The dirt attracts flies, which then lay eggs, which hatch into disgusting little maggots, which in turn feed on their host, starting at the tail, working up, crawling inside the lamb and, eventually, eating the poor creature alive. It is a truly horrific sight, and one I am desperate to avoid. I hate long tails with a passion. All of the tail below the orange ring will die and drop off, leaving a nice short one. As I perform the task, I reassure each lamb that the loss of its tail is for the best, and they don't seem too bothered. Then I mark the lambs with a spray—as well as a number, this pair get a blue B for 'bad mother'. If the ewe should misplace them (and I can't help but feel it is likely) then I can reunite them.

By the time I have gone through all the individual pens, a few more ewes have lambed. It's just before eight and I'm penning a new family as Liam arrives.

'Alreet?'

'Yeah, good thanks. How about you?'

'Aye not bad. Hey, you sound miles better today. Mind, your voice isn't so sexy, like.'

'Get away with you!'

He casts an eye over the shed. 'Many last night?'

'About thirty.'

'How's Ike?'

Ike is Liam's pet lamb. Its mother died in labour and he's become rather attached to it, which I find both funny and quite cute.

'Ike's fine. You can go and feed him and the pet lambs now if you want.'

'Cool.' He heads off towards the little hut where we keep the kettle, milk and bottles as well as all the other lambing paraphernalia.

My job now is to free up some of these pens. I go

back into each of them and check the lambs that I sprayed earlier one more time, just to make sure my previous judgement was sound and that they are indeed ready for the great outdoors. All being well, I pick up each lamb by its front legs, one in each hand, and make my way out of the shed. Because the ewes are Mules, with a strong maternal instinct, they will be hot on my tail, crying after us. To ensure that they keep following me, I imitate a lamb's bleat. I actually reckon I've become quite good at it over the years, but to anyone who happened to stumble upon me, I must look like a right plonker.

Meh meh meeeeh,' I cry as I go, and it works a treat. I carry the lambs down to one of the three small fields by the sheds. They look bewildered at first, standing on wobbly limbs that have only been in use for a few hours. But the mother knows her job and urgently nudges them towards her, running a short distance away then coming back to encourage them to follow. The small field has plenty of shelter and is ideal to get the lambs used to their new outdoor existence before they go into a larger field tomorrow. There is also less chance of them losing their mother in a field this size. The ewe is the lambs' lifeline, and they stand no chance of survival without her. Lambs grow very quickly and by the time tomorrow comes I won't have to carry them to their destination; they will be what farmers call 'footed', able to keep up with their mothers more easily. Once a lamb is footed its chances of survival are very good, but these first few days are crucial. Predators present the main hazard at this stage, but even just losing its mother in the field can be catastrophic. If a ewe loses a lamb for too long in the first few days of its life she is liable to forget that it is hers when it is returned and can sometimes reject it.

I carry on with this job until all of the families I have deemed ready to face the world are outside enjoying the sharp spring air. Their empty pens will be filled with new occupants before I know it.

*　　　*　　　*

Saturday, and it's been a long and gruelling day. Most girls my age would be looking forward to a night out but every fibre of my being is focused on heading home to a hot meal, a big mug of tea and an early night. Roy and Alfie help to keep me nice and toasty in the car, but the thought of slinking into my cosy kitchen and putting the day's worries behind me is simply bliss.

It's been raining all day and it still hasn't stopped. I dash from the car into the farmhouse, my tummy rumbling, thinking about all the treats I deserve and have earned. I flick the light switch. Nothing happens. Oh please, not now.

A quick trip outside reveals the problem. I left the generator on when I went out this morning and it has run out of fuel. I am completely without power until I can refill the tank and bleed the diesel through. Now, what was it that Uncle Toffa said to me when I told him I had no mains electricity here? 'Emma, lass— never, *ever*, let the generator run out of diesel—it'll be a right pain to get it going again.'

So commences an epic night at Fallowlees during which I rail against the generator, my farm, my family, *the cruel, cruel world* and, finally, my idiotic self for being the only one to blame for the frustrating fiasco. The night goes something like this:

116

[20.00 hours]   Fill the tank up

[20.15]   Toddle off in the pouring rain to the generator house

[20.17]   Skid on something and end up on my bottom

[20.18]   Remember the oil filter exploded the week before

[20.19]   Realise that I'm now covered in the stuff

[20.30]   Ring Dad but get no answer

[20.35]   Ring Uncle Toffa and he tries to talk me through the procedure

[20.50]   Discover that my only spanner doesn't quite fit

[20.55]   Question why I never bought another spanner

[21.10]   Realise I have been loosening the wrong bolts

[21.20]   Try ringing Dad again and he tries to talk me through it

[21.35]   Get so frustrated, ask Dad if he can come and help

[21.36]   'You choose to live there, you let the generator dry . . .'

[21.37]   '. . . and I'm busy with lambing, or have you forgotten that?'

[21.39]   Air turns blue after I've put the phone down

[21.45]   Try to ring Uncle Toffa again but my phone dies

[21.49]   Realise I've lost the spanner in the pitch dark generator house

[21.50]   Cry and scream for a bit

[21.53]   Commence a fingertip search of the whole generator house

[21.59]	Find the spanner
[22.03]	Use a bit of metal to make the spanner fit
[22.07]	Wrench the nut with a big metal bar because it is tight with rust
[22.13]	Finally manage to loosen the nut and bleed the generator
[22.30]	Try to restart it. Try to restart it again. And again
[22.35]	And again
[22.36]	The battery is dead. I get the car to jump start it
[22.56]	The generator kicks into life—noisy rattly music to my ears!
[23.00]	It's still raining, I'm frozen to the core. I am beyond caring. I am a genius!
[23.30]	Feed the dogs—gulp long-awaited cup of tea—bed—sleep like the dead
[05.00]	My alarm goes off. A brand new day!

*   *   *

Lambing is a very physical activity, and every day Liam and I have to catch dozens of sheep, for all kinds of reasons. Sheep are large, heavy creatures and they do not like to be caught; they are prey animals, after all, and have no idea if they are going to come off better or worse for these encounters. This is the time of year when the dogs really come into their own. The everyday work they do throughout the year is nothing compared to the bravery and skill required of them at lambing time. They also have to be capable of taking on every situation and adapting to it, no matter what.

Fly's greatest talent is moving ewes and lambs out

into the nursery paddocks. Ewes are at their most aggressive at this time of year and often react to any potential threat with a violent head butt—and take it from me, they pack quite a punch. Fly will walk behind the ewes, but as soon as they turn to face her she will stand stock still. More often than not the mother will test her with a threatening foot stamp and perhaps a lunge, but Fly will hold her ground, waiting patiently for the ewe to realise that she is not in danger. Then the ewe will turn back and start walking once more. Sheep well treated by dogs remember them and I am sure that the flock at Fairspring know and trust my dogs as much as they do me; we have earned it by handling them with care and paying them due respect. The sheep are, after all, our bread and butter. If I were to define my job, their care and wellbeing would be top of my list.

Fly is also very good at catching lambs that have become separated from their mothers or are in need of some treatment. It is important to do this as quickly and as gently as possible. I could run after a lamb all day long and never catch it, as they are surprisingly fast critters even when they are only a few days old; but Fly is like greased lightning. One word from me and she is after the troublesome creature; she steers it close to me, knocks it to the ground and lies over it until I pick it up. There is no real stress on either side.

*   *   *

I go to the shed to check on a ewe who is due to have twins, and who has been pressing on for some time. She has made a little nest of straw in the corner and is busy pawing the ground when

I approach. She turns and looks at me, wary, but doesn't shift from her spot. I manage a peek at her tail end and am worried when there is nothing to see. She has been trying for a long time; something must be wrong. I slowly tiptoe towards her and her eyes and ears flick. She backs up against the wall. I get closer and closer, then make my move and pounce on her, grabbing her abundant woolly coat. My grip is not terrific and she drags me a few yards before I can get my hand under her chin to control her. This girl will weigh at least eighty kilos, and despite her increased girth she is very strong. However, once I have my hand under her chin I have control. Sheep are like horses in this respect: if you control the head the rest of the body will follow suit. I carefully turn her head towards her tail to put her off balance and she falls at my feet. I take off my jacket and place it over her head to keep her still and relaxed, then move round to the business end of her tail and roll up my sleeves.

There is nothing but slime showing outside her vulva. I carefully insert my hand, and it slips easily into the warm wetness. In a healthy presentation, I would be feeling a nose and toes but instead I feel a tail; it is a malpresentation: left like this the lamb will wedge in the birth canal and die. It might eventually be stillborn and discarded by the exhausted ewe; in the worst-case scenario, it can become stuck and lead to the death of the mother, too. Thankfully, a simple procedure will correct it. I slide in my arm as far as I can (luckily I have small hands and terribly skinny wrists) and feel my way down the lamb's rump. I find its leg and reach for a foot, grasp it and pull it in towards me. It pops into the birth canal and sticks out of the ewe's vulva. Meanwhile, the ewe is straining

120

and contracting. I then go in for the other leg, find it easily enough, and now we have a pair of protruding legs. I take a leg in each hand and pull downwards. In one smooth movement the lamb comes away from the safety of the womb that has been his home for 147 days. He jams for a few seconds at his shoulders, then slips out into the world. The white newborn lies motionless for a few seconds before the shock of the cold air motivates him into life. He sneezes and shakes his head vigorously, and his back legs thrash wildly, kicking away the slime near his twitching black nose and thus helping to keep his airways clear. I pull a piece of wool from his mother's fleece and wipe it across his nostrils. He is breathing regularly now, no worse for his ordeal. While the ewe is still lying down I make the most of the opportunity and feel around to see how the other lamb is doing. There is loads more room inside her now that number one is out. I find two little feet and a nose, go to grasp a slippery foot but it doesn't want to meet the world yet and is snatched away from me.

'Oh no you don't,' I tell it, and as the ewe contracts, she pushes the reluctant lamb within my reach and I pull him into the birth canal. He's in a perfect position now, his nose and feet showing, and I pull with the same smooth motion. Out he comes to join his brother.

I move the twins to meet their mother, placing them close to her face, and prepare to lift my coat to reveal the slimy duo to her. She is chuckling and purring at them already and the second I remove the coat she gets straight down to licking them. I watch the little family for a while. The ewe doesn't even look at me: her whole world is lying in front of her. She couldn't be more enthusiastic as she cleans them, and all the while she carries on muttering and reassuring her offspring. It is nothing short of a miracle for such a selfish creature to turn so suddenly into a responsible, caring mother, and I have no doubt that she will defend them against anything.

During these first few minutes of life the ewe will build a bond with her lambs and they with her. As she carries on licking them, the lambs begin to stagger to their feet, moving instinctively towards her udder and its life-giving colostrum. It does not seem to matter that I have seen this any number of times before, each time the sight remains fascinating to me. I would stay there, but I have to get on. There may be sheep in the other sheds who need me. I pick up the still slippery twins by their front legs and carry them across to a freshly bedded individual pen. The ewe follows, agitated that I am moving her precious newborns, and barges in behind me, bleating indignantly as I place them in the pen. She stands protectively over them while I check she is milking on both sides. Sure enough, milk fires from both teats. I then give each lamb an oral dose of antibiotics; the yellow fluid will not taste very nice but they don't object. Finally, I dip their navels into a strong iodine solution to prevent any disease that might use them as a route in. Now it's time to leave them, contented in their own, new little world.

*   *   *

The rain wakes me. No need for the alarm this morning with a noise like that lashing against the window. The sky is still black.

'For fuck's sake!' I exclaim to the view. 'Shit, bugger bollocks!' This is no good. I think of all the tiny lambs outside in this. Their little coats might be waterproof, but they are still terribly thin and vulnerable and can perish in this sort of weather.

At least my cold has dried up. An hour later I'm at Fairspring, wading through muddy puddles as I head for the sheds, looking out for Houdini as I go. Once again, she's not where she should be and I figure she must be somewhere out the back.

'It didn't stop all night,' says Hilary when I find her, gesturing at the scene around us. A raging torrent has come sweeping down the field and been diverted through the central passageway into the shed. All of the straw is damp, some of it soaked completely. The concrete floor where we feed the sheep is nearly a foot deep with water, the wooden troughs bobbing around in it.

Christ, what am I going to do . . . The sheep are still lambing and I am fast running out of pens. They will need feeding soon, too, and I don't think they're going to want to swim for their breakfast. I haven't even had a proper look outside yet. I'm almost afraid at what I might find.

I ring Liam. He sounds croaky with sleep. I apologise for calling him so early but I am going to need all the help I can get.

When I've done the rounds with Hilary, I go looking for Houdini again. She's not in the sheds or hanging around outside them. I have a nagging suspicion she might have gone to give birth somewhere quiet, but it doesn't bear thinking about. I feel anxious as I get out the quad bike and trailer and set off with Roy to find her.

I have to bow my head against the driving force of the rain. At least Roy gets to shelter behind my back although I bet my jacket doesn't smell too good, coated as it is with the effluvia of lambing. Not that he seems to mind.

An open gate leads into the rougher field, a paddock full of brush and rushes. I think I spot something at the far end and as we get closer I realise that my instincts are right: I can just make out a ewe standing close to two white dots.

I park the bike a short distance away then get closer to survey the damage.

'You silly, silly girl,' I tell Houdini.

One lamb is soaked through and trying to shelter from the rain underneath its mother. He looks miserable, and thoroughly sick of the outside world into which he has so unceremoniously landed. He is full of milk, however, and has been well looked after. Lambs can stand some atrocious weather conditions if they have a belly full of good milk.

The other lamb is lying dead a few yards away. The crows have taken an eye already, a trickle of blood running from a tear duct. They perch on the fence post waiting for me to leave so that they can return to feast on the little carcass.

'You silly, silly girl,' I am angrier now. 'Look what you've done! You just wouldn't learn, would you. Whose fault do you think this is?'

I pick up her little survivor and Houdini follows me as I carry him to the trailer. Then I return for his dead sibling, waving and shouting at the crows as I do. I scoop up the frozen body and am just wondering if it is worth skinning it (we sometimes place a skinned fleece on an orphan lamb so that a ewe might accept it as her own), when it opens its mouth and issues a long, barely audible bleat.

'Oh Christ, you poor thing!' Abandoned to the crows, unfed, barely licked clean by its mother, yet still clinging to life. He has lost an eye, for sure. I examine his mouth, as the crows will sometimes take the tongue as well and such lambs are better put down. But no, his tongue is still intact. Survival for this little mite is as long a shot as I've known; but since he is such a proven fighter I decide I have to give him the best possible chance of pulling through. I nestle him on my lap and drive back to the shed.

Liam has turned up and is about to visit his beloved Ike.

'Here, can you put these two in a pen, please, while I try to sort out this little one.'

Liam approaches, sees the grisly sight and recoils in horror.

'Yuck, it's got no eye.' He comes back for a closer look. 'You sure it's still alive?'

The wet body in my arms has indeed gone slack; the head hangs limply. I touch the tear duct on the good eye and get a tiny reflex.

'Yeah, but only just.' I slip a finger inside his mouth to gauge his body temperature. He is icy cold. *You*, I tell it silently, *are going to take some saving*.

I boil the kettle and lay him in the warming box, which is designed to keep air at body temperature. I open the lid and the warm blast hits me in the face. Bliss! I could do with one of these myself. Then I take a large syringe and a clean needle and draw ten millilitres of pure glucose into the vial followed by another ten of boiling water. This means that the contents of the syringe are at exact body temperature. I hold the lamb by his front legs and inject the mixture straight into his abdomen. It will deliver a huge hit of energy, and perhaps help him to pull through. A jab of antibiotics and a painkiller next, and then I lay him gently in the box.

'It's up to you now, little one.'

Later that morning I find Houdini settled in a pen with her other lamb, who looks much happier in his new surroundings.

'Just wait till you see the sunshine,' I tell the little creature. 'You won't know what's hit you.'

It might be a while yet, though. Through the shed door I can see the families that were turned out earlier in the week standing close to the wall, their backs to the rain. I go back to check on the one-eyed waif, prepared for the worst. When I open the lid I am in for a surprise. He has come round and is actually sitting up, his head raised.

'Hey, well done, Popeye!' I tell him.

Liam peeps over my shoulder. 'Yuck,' he says again. 'Look at that eye.'

It's true—the eye is grotesque, and the whole left side of his face is a mess of congealed blood.

'I reckon he's ready for some milk now,' I say.

Liam looks at me and smiles. 'Jordan?'

'Yep, Jordan it is.'

Jordan the sheep is something of a legend here at Fairspring. Like all the ewes in lamb, her udder began to grow steadily larger day by day at the start of the season, and her belly grew too in direct proportion. Unlike the other ewes, she didn't seem to want to ever *stop* growing. Every day we would marvel at her size and swear she must have reached capacity . . . but she would confound us, again and again, and still without signs of lambing.

Until yesterday . . .

Yesterday, Jordan outdid herself and gave birth to four enormous lambs. She had been scanned for three, but given her size I suppose we should have predicted an extra one.

I jump into Jordan's pen armed with an empty jug, tip her over and start to milk her. As I squeeze the teat rhythmically, thick, yellowish colostrum shoots out. Liam is wandering around, filling the knocked-over water buckets and topping up hay supplies. I sit the jug, now full of warm, foamy milk, on the side.

'Here, come and see,' I call to him. My protégé comes bouncing over, always keen to learn something new.

He leans over the pen. 'What?'

At that exact moment I fire a perfect jet of milk right at his face. He squeals with fright and immediately puts his hand to his well-maintained quiff.

'Me hair! This look takes time, ya kna. I'll get you for this.'

Then we both collapse with laughter. He fills a syringe with water, firing it at me as I climb out of the pen. I scream and run for cover, both of us still laughing hysterically. I doubt whether we would normally have found something so simple so entertaining, but things are different at lambing time. We are all tired, we are all under pressure and if we didn't keep a good sense of humour we would probably all go mad.

I take Popeye out of the warming box and hold him lightly at my knees. He is already much stronger, but unable to suck properly. I dip one end of a tube into the jug of milk then slide it into the corner of his mouth and all the way down into his stomach. I then draw up a big fat syringe of milk, attach it to the tube, and slowly and carefully depress the plunger until the syringe is empty. I repeat this three times, as poor little Popeye is starving. I can see his little tummy filling up as I do it. Colostrum is only produced for the first few days after giving birth and it is vital that a lamb—or any young mammal—gets a good dose early on. Not only is it full of fat, it is also rich in essential antibodies that are not found in the milk that comes later. Then back he goes in the warming box while I get on with other tasks.

*   *   *

It has been a long, long day and I can hardly describe how relieved I am to see Hilary poke her head round the corner. The last hour has been a mad dash to get everything shipshape for her. The ewes have been fed and watered, their lambs are feeding well, the pet lambs have all been bottle fed. The empty pens are ready for new families during the night. Liam and I are constantly toing and froing throughout the day, which can be quite disturbing to the sheep, but when we have settled for the day, they settle too and almost every one of them is now lying down contentedly. Here and there a ewe will have her chin resting on the ground, fast asleep. If you watch very carefully you can see them dreaming, their eyelids twitching, an ear sometimes flapping away a non-existent fly. I wonder what sheep dream of. Summer pastures? The tup that fathered their children? I reckon the majority will be dreaming of their stomachs—lush grass and tasty treacle concentrates, oats and beans and barley.

We do our rounds, and pause by the pet-lamb pen. Liam's Ike is big and fat now, and when he sees us he gets to his feet bleating a welcome, pretending he hasn't been fed.

'Crafty devils, aren't they,' says Hilary. 'Who says sheep are stupid?'

When I catch sight of myself in the rear view

mirror of banana car, I'm a little shocked. A cold sore has left an angry mark on my bottom lip. The skin around my nose is still red and peeling from my cold. In fact, my whole face is dry and raw. There is a splash of iodine dangerously close to my right eye, my hair has formed its own dreadlocks—it's crusty with colostrum—and to cap it all I have bags under my eyes. I'm not a pretty picture. If I were to sit on a street corner people would throw money at me!

Who's going to fancy me these days? I wonder if Liam does! We certainly have a good laugh together, not a bad basis for a relationship. I doubt he does, though. He clearly cares about appearance so I bet he has a girlfriend with tidy hair and manicured fingernails and pretty perfume and neat clothes.

Sometimes I imagine the farmers discussing me at the mart. 'Aye, that Emma Gray, you must have heard of her. Used to be quite a bonny lass—bit of a livewire, too, till she got that farm . . . She all but lost her looks *and* her marbles, never seemed to laugh. Lives all by herself with a coupla sheep and a load of dogs—barking mad, they say.'

I cackle to myself, then think, 'Crikey, I *am* going mad!'

As soon as I'm home I run a deep, hot bubble bath and wash away all the signs of lambing.

Chapter Eight

Not much longer to go now, I think, as I drag myself out of bed. These five o'clock starts are killing me, and what with the strenuous nature of lambing and the long drive to work, I feel permanently knackered.

Liam is there already, which must be a first.

He laughs as I park the banana car.

'Only a lass could drive a thing like that.'

'Admit it, you're warming to her.'

'Hadaway, man!'

'You drove her yesterday.'

'Only cos you let us off for half a second to fetch some chocolate from the shop.'

We make a good team, Liam and me. He's been so willing to learn. I can hardly believe he is the same guy who had eyes only for tractors a few weeks ago. We go off to do our separate tasks, but a little later that morning he comes to find me.

'Did you know there's a single on lambing in there?'

My observational skills have clearly been slipping. This is what we've been waiting for and I hadn't twigged. I follow him into the shed. We move quietly across to the pen holding all the single-bearing ewes. Sure enough, there she is, tucked away in the corner. She's a big, powerful-looking girl.

'Let's catch and separate her and see if she's got plenty of milk,' I say.

We sidle up to the ewe, who looks at us warily. The rest of the flock in the pen are unconcerned; they have seen us making idiots of ourselves many times before as we try to catch one—and by now they are quick to work out when we're on to them. I've tried everything: sidling up to them, not looking them in the eye, not talking to them, talking nicely to them, and none of these tactics is failsafe. The element of surprise will not make a blind bit of difference. We edge closer now. The ewe, aware she is being boxed in, makes a bolt for it. Liam dives and grabs a good handful of wool but the ewe takes him with her and clatters him off a metal support. He holds on with a determination he certainly didn't possess at the start of lambing. I watch as he guides the ewe towards an empty pen. He straddles her like a horse but without putting any weight on her back, steering her by moving her head. She is now in the pen, with minimal stress for either party. I feel a bit proud as I watch my assistant be so competent.

'Right, let's see how you're milking.' I jump into the pen and feel her vast udder. Sometimes a ewe will only milk on one side, which is no good if she has more than one lamb, but this girl is firing on both sides.

'There's enough milk in there for Elizabeth Taylor to have a bath,' I tell Liam.

'Eh?'

'Oh never mind,' I say and check how far through her labour she is. The nose and front feet are nearly out.

'She's been on lambing a while. Lucky you spotted her. A few minutes later and we would have missed her. Go and get one of the pet lambs.'

Liam disappears and I tip the ewe on to her side ready to deliver her newborn. Liam comes back empty handed.

'No pets left?'

He shrugs. 'Just Popeye.'

'Well bring Popeye then.'

'Not Popeye, he's me mate.'

'Liam, this ewe is Popeye's best chance. You know that, don't you?'

He looks crestfallen. 'Yeah I suppose.' He slopes off and returns with the lamb in his arms. Popeye has come on in leaps and bounds since his birth. He is as full as a gun and as frisky as, well, a lamb.

'Now, go and get a bucket of warm water.'

Liam hands Popeye to me and off he goes again.

I look at the ravaged face and feel a surge of affection for this tough little creature. If my plan works, this ewe will be a far better mother to him than Houdini ever was. I tie his legs together with some string to immobilise him and, when Liam comes back with the water, dip Popeye in it and lie him behind the ewe. Naturally he's not too impressed and puts up a struggle. Next, I gently ease out the legs of the unborn lamb. They pop into place, closely followed by a head. She's a big one but with one smooth movement she slides over Popeye and out into the world. Now, Liam and I rub as much birth fluid as we can into Popeye. We even rub the newborn's legs and tail over our one-eyed reject, covering him with the ewe's scent. When we are satisfied, we pick up the newborn and lift her out of the pen for now. She is obviously a little bewildered, poor thing, coming into this world and finding things not quite as she might have expected.

The ewe gets to her feet. All of her instincts are screaming out for a lamb right now. She sees Popeye and gives him a tentative sniff, then a lick, and then another. In next to no time she is licking him all over, muttering to him as if he were her own. His legs are tied so that he behaves like a minutes-old lamb—a supposed newborn jumping straight to its feet can make the mother suspicious and we don't want to scupper our plans. After a few minutes we drop her real lamb back in the pen, and untie Popeye's legs. He jumps to his feet and nudges his new mother for a drink. The ewe has bonded with him and allows him to feed while she licks the other lamb clean.

Liam and I look at the three creatures in front of us.

'Well, I bet our little friend will never look back,' I say. 'What a great mother she's going to be.'

Liam is slightly more subdued, but he nods his head. 'Aye. I suppose you're right.'

*   *   *

Now that things are calming down at work I can start to resurrect my social life. Nikki and I went to Otterburn Tower, a hotel not far from me, and I had more to drink than I care to remember. The next day she rings me.

'Guess what. I've just had a text from Chris—from last night? He says "Hi, I think Emma is really hot. Can you send me her number?"'

'Eek!'

'*Well*? What do you think, Em . . . do you want me to send it?'

'I dunno that I can even remember who Chris is!'

'He was the one at the end of the bar who was staring at you all night of course.'

'No! He wasn't, was he?'

Nikki laughs. 'No, not really. He was the guy with Nigel, with the striped shirt.'

'Ah yes, him. What does he do?'

'I think he drives tractors. I don't really know him

133

but he seems nice enough. I had his number through some stuff I was doing at Young Farmers. So . . . do you want me to send him yours?'

'I don't know, Nikki. I don't even know him.'

'Well there's nothing to lose.'

'Go on, then; you might as well.'

*   *   *

I am doing the early morning drive round the fields to see how all the sheep there are faring. The shed is all in control, and I have left Liam in charge back there. I cast a quick eye over the seventy Blackfaces in the lambing field, a breed I have not worked with before. New sheep are at a premium, the prices can be painful, so rather than buying in two-year-old Mules, Michael has decided to buy the flock of Blackfaces and cross-breed from them instead.

From the start, these wild hill sheep have given me the run around. They never seem to be in the field they are supposed to be in and I feel sorry for the two Leicesters we bought to mate with them. If I so much as step foot in their field they tend to dash off to the far corner, quite unlike my lovely Mules who have always seemed like house pets in comparison.

Initially I had brought the Blackfaces inside to lamb, but they were unhappy and spent the whole time pining, never settling for a moment and picking at their feed. So I decided they would be better off outside. In spite of the terrible weather and their heavy, full-term bellies, they had managed to make their way to the highest, most windswept field on the farm, and it was only there that they were happy again. They seemed to manage well. I drove round them three times a day, and at each visit there would be another crop of lambs, usually already on their feet and feeding. The lambs themselves are delightfully pretty, and they have amazing get up and go about them. Mules are sheep royalty in my book; I can hardly wait to watch them grow up and give birth to their own lambs in turn.

Today, as I do my drive through, I feel that something is different. At the far end of the field a white lamb lies prone, the mother not far away. The lamb is dead, cloudy-eyed. It never drew a breath—perhaps the thin film of the birth sac was over its face, suffocating the poor creature. The ewe looks fit and well, though, and will make a good mother, so I open the trailer door and use her dead lamb to try to lure her inside. I make pathetic-sounding 'meh-meh' noises, but she is not fooled. While Mules are trusting and well behaved and would have trotted into my trailer without a backward glance, the Blackfaces are wily, difficult and positively truculent.

'Right, you had your chance,' I say. 'We'll do it the hard way, then.'

Roy has been waiting on the bike like a coiled spring. At a word he shoots off to gather her. The ewe runs off in fright, but Roy blocks her every turn. Closer and closer she comes, trying to break free. Roy stops her and backs her towards me. The ewe grows weary and stands there, stamping her feet at the approaching dog. I take the opportunity while her back is turned to make a dive for her, grabbing a handful of wool just as Roy makes a jump for the wool under her neck. She can't resist now.

'Good boy, Roy! On the bike!' He bounds away, happy as Larry. Catching sheep is his favourite job!

I drag the reluctant ewe to the trailer, tying her horn to its side—I learnt my lesson after I put a

135

Blackface in the trailer only to discover when I got back to the sheds that she had escaped en route.

Back at the sheds I drag the ewe into a pen, (the horns are occasionally of benefit) before I then take the dead lamb to the skinning post outside. With my penknife I slit the skin round each of its back legs, joining the split to the other side, and work it away from the pale pink flesh. Once it is clear I pull it firmly away from the body. It pulls well right down to the lamb's head and forelegs where I cut it free, producing a little jacket from the dead creature. It looks a sorry sight now, but it is all for the greater good. In the pet-lamb pen I find a lamb of a similar size and fit the jacket over it, head through the head hole, legs through the leg holes, like dressing a child. Then I go to introduce the 'reincarnated' lamb to its mother.

Or would have if the pen were not empty. Damn. I might have known it.

I ask Liam if he's seen it about and he answers from the other side of the shed that yes, he has, and he has put her in another pen.

'And I've put another hurdle on top to stop her jumping out,' he adds matter of factly.

Now, why didn't I think of that? Liam's a smart cookie; he's always surprising me with new initiatives like this.

I give the lamb to its new mother. She perks up right away at the sight of the fluffy bundle. An hour ago it was lying unmoving and now it is frisky as you like. She sniffs it, then sniffs it again, a bit unsure— which means it is time to call in Alfie. I stand next to the pen and ask Alfie to 'watch her'. He stands and looks at her. The ewe's urge to protect her offspring suddenly kicks in. Muttering to the lamb she stamps her foot at Alfie, daring him to come any closer. Alfie is used to this job and he is great at it. He doesn't budge. By now the little lamb has cottoned on to its surrogate mum, has found her teat and is helping itself to breakfast.

Ten minutes later and the ewe is happily settled with what she thinks is her own lamb. The bond created in the first day lasts until the lambs are weaned. Even after I have removed the skin in a day or so, this lamb will be bonded to the ewe through thick and thin.

*   *   *

Even though lambing seems to have gone on for ever, it comes as a surprise that it's almost over. Today, for the first time in ages, the sun is shining and it warms me right to the core.

Hilary finished her night shift reporting that no lambs were born and she even managed to snatch a few hours' sleep, to get herself back into a normal routine. The shed is virtually empty now. The daily battle to keep the pens empty and get the ewes and new lambs outside is over for another year. Today there are only around twenty ewes milling about in each shed; they have all the room in the world and many of the individual pens are open and will no longer be required.

Sun streams in through the open side of the shed and the relaxed ewes doze in the strips of sunlight that warm up the floor. Everywhere smells earthy and fresh, the mud is finally drying in the yard and the rain we saw so much of seems a distant memory.

I hop on the bike and set off to check the sheep feeling everything is right with the world and that nothing could possibly go wrong. I'm feeling a bit giddy; shepherdess is the best job there could possibly be. Bill sits beside me and Roy jogs along beside the bike until I come to the first gate. He uses this temporary stop as an excuse to hop on too. He might be the best sheepdog but he's never been one for unnecessary exercise!

The daffodils at the roadside, which were only green spears a few weeks ago, have blossomed into yellow trumpets. The lambs are full and contented and many are lying down dozing in the sun. A few of them are using the weather as an excuse for games, galloping along the fence line and stopping every so often for a quick head-butt battle.

Each field is the same, dotted with happy families. I can see all the familiar faces from lambing time: Popeye and his adoptive sister lie together while their mother grazes nearby. He looks healthy and the missing eye will give him no problems. Sheep are remarkably adaptable. In the same field is the ewe I marked B for 'bad mother'. Those skinny little lambs are filling out nicely. Calcium ewe, marked with a big red C, is over in the next field. I have kept an eye on her but the symptoms did not recur. She was not the only sheep to suffer from milk fever this year and I make a mental note to check the feed ration to stop it happening again next year.

I finish in the highest field on Fairspring, the Blackface field. Even they seem contented and settled now they are getting used to me and the farm, and although some blare for their lambs as I pass by, most are happy to let me drive through. Their little mottled-face Mule offspring are the future for Fairspring. I get off the bike and sit down in the growing grass. Bill and Roy hop off too. Bill goes off looking for moles while Roy sits nearby. I look across the farm, at all the happy little white dots grazing or snoozing under the puffy clouds and blue sky. The traumas of lambing are forgotten. This one moment makes it all worthwhile.

*   *   *

It is nice to be home at a decent time, walking the dogs while it's still light. This is good thinking time, when I wonder about life, both the big things and the little things, everything from world politics to what I'm going to make for tea. Today, I think, a nice bolognaise is on the cards. I am lost in a little reverie of cooking smells and yummy things when my phone beeps. It's Chris.

'U OK?' reads his text.

'Fine,' I text back. 'What up to?'

So begins a succession of text messages. We correspond back and forth over the next couple of days, quite enjoying the conversation. He seems to be a good laugh. Perhaps this will work.

*   *   *

Rejoice! I have my five Suffolks back. At first they were like wild creatures! I spotted them one evening close to the farm, when Fly, Roy and Alfie were all with me, and this time the sheep had no option. Once we had them back home, it was like having a herd of deer. For the first few days, they were horribly nervous of the dogs and me but the sight of that sweet green delicious grass helped them realise they were on to a good thing.

Today I have to be home for the carpet fitters, and

they turn up in their van, scratching their heads as they look at the house and back at the way they've come.

'I never would have believed anyone lived up here if you hadn't given us them instructions,' says the older man. His accomplice, a gangly youth, nods his agreement.

'It reminds us of that Hannah Hauxwell woman, but you'll be too young to remember her,' he adds.

If I had a penny for everyone who mentioned Hannah Hauxwell . . .

I reply, 'Oh I know all about Hannah. She was pretty amazing. My life is luxurious compared to hers.'

I leave the men to get on with the job, making cups of tea as required. I hear them all morning, banging away (and hope my house can withstand it).

I take Alfie out for a run on the sheep and the men come out to watch. I quite enjoy having spectators, and ones like this, who have never seen anything quite like it, are always suitably impressed. After Alfie, I decide to give Len a go. I haven't had the opportunity to do much with him recently, what with lambing and with no sheep of my own for so long. I put him on the long lead again so that I have got some control, but I trust him enough now not to use the muzzle.

'He's just a young dog,' I tell my audience. 'Too young to train properly but he's so keen. I don't overdo it though.'

Len has the devil in him this morning. Forgetting all he's been taught he dashes straight in and cuts off one of the small flock. As he runs round the ewe she trips on the rope, it tightens, and Len, too, gets it caught between his legs. The next thing I know, both he and the unfortunate creature are tied together on the ground, neither of them able to get up.

It's a comical sight, and I turn to the carpet fitters, shaking my head in exasperation. But they only look more impressed than ever.

The young lad's mouth is hanging open. 'Whey, I never would have believed it if I hadn't seen it with me own eyes. I knew them dogs were clever, but how the hell do you teach them to tie up a sheep?'

*   *   *

It always cheers me up driving through the forest at night. In the early days here I found the tall swaying trees frightening and a little spooky, their long limbs like arms warning me to stay away. But so much has changed since, and now they seem welcoming, as familiar to me as my own furniture. I think of them as *my* trees in *my* very own forest. Tonight I am on my way home from a disastrous night out and these trees are like an instant hug.

Chris and I had arranged to meet at a restaurant that he assured me was halfway between our homes. It had taken me far longer to get there than I'd expected, and I pulled up outside fifteen minutes late. I ran inside, apologies at the ready, but slightly miffed that he had suggested somewhere far easier for him to get to than for me.

I saw a nice-looking guy sitting on his own over in the corner, and beamed at him. There was no one else in the bar. He looked a bit perplexed and a second later his wife or girlfriend rejoined him. I felt like an idiot. Luckily, the waiter whisked them quickly off to seat them at their table, so I didn't have to suffer the embarrassment of perching on my own beside them.

141

Chris wasn't there. The waiter suggested I have a drink at the bar while I was waiting and I ordered an orange juice, then instantly regretted it. I had a nagging feeling I'd been stood up, and I wouldn't be able to make a quick getaway now. I looked at my watch. How long would I give him?

Ten minutes later, just as I was deciding I'd finish my drink and leave, a man appeared at my shoulder and asked if I was Emma. Somehow I managed a smile and accepted his apologies.

'Yours isn't that Lexus outside, is it?' he asked as we took our seats in the restaurant.

I laughed. 'No, I've just got a cheap old run-around. The one that looks like a banana.'

He looked relieved. 'Mine's that midnight blue BMW over the road.' He pointed outside. 'With the alloy wheels and the tinted windows.'

I flashed a quick glance to the window. 'Oh. Nice.'

'Yeah, she runs like a dream. I got her second-hand, of course, but people who own BMs take care of their cars and she's as good as new. One careful company director owner.' He laughed. 'Very nice wood trim inside, too.'

'Hey, driving a tractor must be a lucrative job!' I joked. 'I always knew I was in the wrong profession.'

He looked hurt. 'I won't pretend I earn the best wage in the world. I do work hard though, and I'm careful with my money. That car's my pride and joy. Puts a smile on my face in the mornings.'

Hmm, it didn't sound as if this man needed a woman. A nice machine was clearly all that was required to get *his* motor running.

'The stuffed mushrooms sound nice,' I said, hoping to change the subject.

He glanced briefly at the menu. 'Do you know, my

last car was a VW, and I wondered if I was doing the right thing because it served me well that car, but I'm pleased to say I've never regretted buying the BM.'

I was starting to have a few regrets myself by now. Oh, where was that waiter? I needed a drink, too, an alcoholic one this time. This was going to be a long evening.

About halfway through the main course he changed the subject.

'So, you've got a farm?' A bit of interest in me. Hooray!

I told him I was a shepherd by profession and he pulled a face.

'Must drive you nuts working with sheep all day. Aren't they a bit stupid?'

Oh dear. This guy was a moron. I had a sudden urge to defend my fleecy charges. Should I tell him how they can sometimes surprise you, and display a bit of cunning that takes your breath away? Should I tell him about my beautiful Mules, who could put a few human mothers to shame? Was it worth it? Probably not. Tractor drivers are notorious for not getting on with livestock, and he was just the worst possible example of one.

I looked at my wine glass, now empty, and wished I wasn't driving.

I can't remember what we talked about after that, but when he asked if I wanted dessert I shook my head vigorously and said I really needed to get back to tuck the sheep in for the night.

At least he didn't ask to see me again. I think we both knew it was a disaster.

Two eyes glint at me in the yard as I park the car, and a few seconds later a warm nose is pushed into my hand. 'Roy! How did you get out?'

His kennel is still fastened shut so I'm none the wiser.

'Come on, Roy, in. Time for bed.' I hold the kennel door for him and he sits down and lets out a little whine.

'Oh. OK, you win. I could do with some decent company tonight.' We go inside together, Roy wagging his tail happily. He trots up those steep stairs and makes himself comfortable on the floor beside my bed, as if he did it every night. With his head flat on the floor, he watches me as I brush my teeth and get undressed.

'Oh, Roy, how am I ever supposed to get a man with you in my bedroom?' I laugh. 'Perhaps this is what Chris is like with his car,' I tell him. 'Sorry, not car, the *BM*.'

Roy gives a yawn. 'My feelings entirely. Goodnight, Roy, my gorgeous creature. Who needs a man with a dog like you?'

*   *   *

I am in a field at Fairspring giving Alfie a refresher course and trying not to think about the date from hell. It is late April and all of the sheep have lambed. After lambing the dogs can alter and display inappropriate behaviour after becoming used to dealing with aggressive ewes and I want to correct this before the upcoming trials. Where a sharp bite on the nose of a badly behaved ewe is acceptable at home, on the trials field it would spell the end of the road for the dog. So I am out doing what we call 'polishing', that is, putting the finer points on the dogs' performance. But Alfie, who normally runs like a heat-seeking missile, just isn't

144

himself today.

Alfie may be a bit of an idiot—at the beach he will drink seawater and make himself sick; when chasing a ball he will wait for another dog to pick it up even if he gets there first—but the fact of the matter is, this loveable plonker is an extremely talented sheepdog. He can run for miles without tiring. He has benefited from everything I learned training Bess, Bill, Fly and Roy, and as such I haven't made as many mistakes with him. He stops instantly on a whistle and I can move him anywhere in a field regardless of whether there are any sheep in it, such is his obedience. He also stops on his feet in a stand, giving him more presence. He has no fear of sheep and will march up to any tup or ewe quite happily, but never threaten them. They accept him readily.

Today something's wrong. Today he wanders on a few paces after his stop whistle. I call him back and send him out to the other side to see if there is an improvement, but no, just the same lacklustre performance.

'Oh for God's sake, Alfie, what's up with you?' I mutter and put him back in the car. I take Roy out next and his performance cheers me up no end. He really is a talent—brainy and powerful, perhaps not always the best listener, but he usually knows more than me anyway!

I decide to give Alfie another go. I open the door and call him out. No response. I call again. No response. I look inside the car and Alfie is struggling to get to his feet. When he finally heaves himself up and shuffles out, it is as if I'm looking at a different animal. He can hardly move. He is as stiff and sore as an old dog of fifteen.

'Oh, Alfie, what's wrong?'

He stands there trembling, crying very gently.

*   *   *

Alfie is fading fast. By the time we get to the vet's he can barely walk. He lies flat out in the waiting room to take the pressure off his aching limbs. A woman and her child come out of the consulting room with a black Labrador sporting a lampshade on his head.

'Ah, nice old boy. What age is he?' they say in passing.

'He's not three yet,' I say, sharply. They shuffle on, obviously put out by my tone, but all I can think of is Alfie and what is happening to him. He is not screaming in pain, but I know that he is in agony. I am desperate for him to be seen to. By the time the vet is ready for us I have to carry my poor dog in and lie him on the table.

Angus the vet examines him and asks me the usual questions. How long has he been like this? Has he eaten anything unusual? Is he drinking? What are his movements like? I tell him it is a mystery to me. Alfie is such a healthy, lively dog, and this was the first sign that anything was wrong. I cannot fathom how he can have gone downhill so rapidly. More worryingly, nor can Angus.

As we are unable to pinpoint anything specific, he says he will have to treat broadly using anti-inflammatory painkillers and antibiotics. We agree that I'll leave Alfie with him so that he can monitor the situation. *It doesn't get any easier*, I think to myself, as I drive back to Fairspring.

*   *   *

146

When Bess was injured, all those years ago, I thought I had lost her and perhaps that makes it harder to hope for a happy ending this time— as if twice is pushing it. Each one of my dogs is so important to me, each one bringing his or her own qualities, each of them capable of filling me with pride or making me laugh for a different reason. Alfie is such a comedian; I cannot bear the thought of him dying. Not knowing what is the matter is only making it worse.

By about five p.m. I've decided to call it a day at work. Only one of the lambing sheds is still in operation and there are just a handful of new families getting to know each other in the pens. All looks in order out in the fields, too, and I am making my way to the car when my mobile rings. I just know it will be Angus and my voice is shaking slightly as I answer. When he asks me if there are deer at Fallowlees I am slightly taken aback.

'Deer? Yes, loads of them. I see them most nights when I'm out with the dogs, but they're very nervous of us.'

'It's just that I noticed a couple of ticks on Alfie. They live on deer, you know, and can attach themselves to humans or animals passing through long grass or shrubs. I don't see this very often but I've consulted a few colleagues and done some research and I'm starting to think Alfie might have Lyme disease.'

Alfie has the classic symptoms, apparently. Lethargy, fever, joint and muscle pain. The good thing is that it is treatable and Alfie is already showing some improvement. If he remains stable overnight, I can probably take him home tomorrow.

It is an emotional moment and I am beyond

relieved. It frightened me to see my fit and healthy youngster—and young star—deteriorate so rapidly. The diagnosis has given me something else to worry about, though, something I have never given any thought to before. Long grass, low-hanging branches; all the little blighters that must be hiding in the undergrowth, waiting for something warm-blooded to come along, just so that they can have a good old feed. Nothing seems to be simple, not at the moment, that's for sure.

* * *

A few days later I am at a competition and get talking to one of my fellow competitors, Katy Cropper. I've known Katy for a few years—she used to be married to Jim Cropper, a top sheepdog handler. She asks if I have enough points to compete in the national. To qualify, you need to be placed—and therefore earn points—at open trials held throughout the year. In June the top one hundred and fifty handlers are picked from all of the entries submitted to the International Sheep Dog Society.

I pull a face. 'I don't know if I have, and there are hardly any more trials from now till the cut-off.'

'Well,' says Katy, 'I'm going down to Devon next weekend for a couple of nights. Why don't you come with me? It means you can compete in two trials in a weekend, and it'll be a good laugh.'

I must admit, I like the idea. Alfie is home and recovering well—he hates to be left out of anything and as soon as he had the strength he was up and about with the other dogs and making an exhibition of himself, even though you could tell it was a bit of an effort for him at times. But it means leaving Liam to run the farm on his own, and I wonder if that's fair. I call Mum to see what she thinks.

'The place isn't going to fall apart without you, and it'll be nice to have a break after all the stress of the last few months. You said Liam was quite capable now so leaving him for a day or two won't hurt.'

Katy has it all planned. We're competing in three trials and staying with her friend, the comedian Jethro. Next thing I know I'm flying down the M6 with Katy, her daughter and her daughter's friend. I have all my dogs with me and Katy has her three. I have never been so far south before.

The trial is set over two large fields with a big dip in the bottom. The dogs have to run down the hill, over a stream, then up the hill, through an open gate and across another three hundred yards to the sheep. Many of the people competing know the field and their dogs are familiar with the terrain, but it's all new to us.

Fly spots the sheep straight away and makes a good line to them, jumping the fence rather than taking the easier route of the open gate. The judge consequently disqualifies me. Our next few runs don't go to plan either, but I don't really mind: I'm having a whale of a time.

I have not been anywhere other than Fairspring or Fallowlees for months now, and the change of scene is invigorating. I laugh and joke with other triallers and Katy introduces me to an old friend of hers, Rick. Rick is the creator of something called the Big Sheep. It turns out to be a queer sort of tourist attraction, with sheep racing and sheep rides, and something entirely new to me: *duck herding*.

'It sounds amazing,' I say.

149

'Well, that it is. Why don't you come and work for me as a shepherdess?' says Rick, to my surprise. 'You'd get to work your dogs every day and show off a bit, the dogs would love it, and you'd meet lots of new people. If you don't mind me saying, you're a lively sort, Emma. You're wasted stuck out on a poor farm in Northumberland.'

I'm not sure this is how I see myself, and I feel a bit put out to hear Fallowlees described in these terms, but I know he's genuinely trying to help me.

'I've got a great team and I'm sure you'd love them,' he adds. 'You'd fit in perfectly.'

I have to admit that it does sound appealing. A few months back I would have bitten his hand off for an opportunity like this, a fresh start for me and my dogs. New people, new places. I suppose that he has touched a raw nerve: deep down I'm worried that I'll never make new friends as long as I continue with my rather isolated existence. This weekend has reminded me how much fun life can be when you've got human company. But then I think about Fallowlees. I did not fight as hard as I did to win her only to let her go so soon. I've barely even started to put my plans for the place into practice. I *believe* in Fallowlees. I *belong* there.

'I'm sorry, Rick. It sounds brilliant, and I know I'd love it, but I just can't leave my farm.'

Rick grins. 'I thought you might say that. Let me know if you change your mind.'

As we make our long journey home, I keep harking back to our earlier conversation. I may not be contemplating a move to Devon, but supposing there is a way of taking some of Rick's ideas up north? There's no real reason why they shouldn't work. I could have the best of both worlds. I pass much of the journey in a world of my own.

*   *   *

The first thing I do when I get back is ring Liam. He tells me that five lambs have died while I've been away. It is not unusual for a few of the lambs to die; but five in such a short space of time is alarming.

I rush to the farm early the next morning. Daylight is not far off as I drive through the fields on the quad bike. To my horror, it is not long before I see three lambs lying dead on the ground in front of me. In the last field, I find one of the bad mother's lambs stone cold on the ground. This one had grown big and healthy and I had been proud of the way his mother had taken on her responsibilities. His brother is standing with his mother nearby, looking in good health. On closer examination I find his backside is matted with scour—a thin, watery layer of excrement. This is a sign of nematodirus—easy to cure but lethal if left unchecked. It is a problem usually localised to Northumberland and the Borders. I have heard of farms suffering huge losses to this devastating nematode, which can strike very quickly if the climatic conditions are just right. This year the worm that causes the virus is hatching just as the vulnerable young lambs are starting to graze, meaning one thing is certain: all of the lambs will need to come inside instantly for treatment.

I ring Liam and ask him to come in as soon as possible. Every lamb will need to be treated today if I am to prevent any further deaths. It will be another long day. We will have to bring nearly one thousand ewes and their lambs into the pens in the course of just a few hours. I will need all the skill and stamina

151

of my dogs.

By the time Liam arrives, I have shed the lambs from the ewes and I am preparing the dosing guns. Roy and Bill have been hard at work pushing the sheep through the race so that I can shed them, and both of them are now standing in the water trough cooling off. It is the one job that Bill still loves; he likes to show the younger dogs how it's done from time to time and, to be honest, despite his age he is still the best at pushing those ewes through—a tough job when the lambs are so young.

We make a start on the first lot. Liam and I have a race full of lambs each and we work our way along it, squirting a measured dose through the applicator and into the mouth of each lamb. I wish they knew that we were saving their lives but of course they don't and they are reluctant to swallow. It is the first time they have been handled since lambing time and they are touchy and wriggly at the best of times. We work away, lamb after lamb, field after field. It is practically dark when we prepare to bring in the last batch, the Blackfaces. The dogs are exhausted. I've already used Alfie, but looking at all the others now, I know he's my only hope of finishing this job. He's always had the most stamina, but given he is only just up and running after the Lyme disease I am wavering on deciding whether or not he is fit enough for this further challenge.

'What do you think, Alfie? Are you up to it?'

Alfie certainly thinks he is. He wags his tail and jumps straight out of the car.

'Come on then, let's get these little devils down.'

Alfie draws on everything he's got to bring these cunning hill sheep down from the field. As I watch him tearing around, I can hardly believe that this is

152

the same dog who hardly had the strength to lift his head only a matter of days ago. It is fully dark by the time Liam and I let the horned sheep back into their high field. We are both stiff and sore from our tussles with the twisty little lambs. The dogs stretch out on the back seat of the banana car, filthy but happy. A collie is never happier than when he's tired after a good job done, I think.

'Aye, I think a pint is in order,' announces Liam, having a stretch.

'You're not wrong. Have one for me. I'm off home for an early night.'

I'm exhausted, but relieved that the lambs are safe now. Over the next few days a few lambs look dehydrated and a bit sorry for themselves and I lose two more, but dosing them all quickly has stopped the worms in their tracks. I shouldn't have left them all weekend. I should have guessed something would happen.

Chapter Nine

When Fly finally came in season I lined her to Paul Bristow's dog Bill, who is the father of Roy and Len and a tremendous worker. Naturally I am very excited about the litter and the prospect of a pup with the biddable instinct and loyalty of my favourite dog combined with the working instinct of Roy. I'm going to keep one of the pups to train myself and sell the others, which will hopefully pay for that long-awaited new engine.

I'm resting Fly as much as possible, though I continue to use her for the gentle jobs as she hates being locked away if the other dogs are out with me. She is about two weeks from her due date and starting to fatten up, her teats becoming more prominent.

One morning I go into the kennels and Fly isn't the first dog I see. She is usually there right at the front waiting for me, crying to get out and say hello, her right top lip lifting in that goofy smile that she reserves for me and my family.

Today she is still in her basket. I let the other dogs out and get down beside her and ask her what's wrong. She lifts her head and feebly wags her tail, but doesn't get up. Something's the matter. On closer inspection I can see she is bleeding from her vulva. I wonder if it's pyometra, an infection of the womb common in bitches, that I saw during a spell working as a veterinary nurse in Hexham after I got back from New Zealand. But whatever it is, I fear she is losing the puppies.

I get straight on the phone to Angus the vet and tell him I'm bringing her in. I can't get to the surgery quickly enough. Angus is bemused. He can see with his ultrasound scanner that Fly has five pups, but all he knows is that something is not right. As he examines her, Fly lies on her back, holding her back leg in the air out of the way to make it easier for him.

I am terribly disappointed that this pregnancy is going to end. I shouldn't have let myself get so excited about it, but I do it every time. I tell myself to be philosophical; after all, I know from working with livestock for so long that these things happen. Fly is still young, she will have more opportunities. This just wasn't the right time. Angus asks me to leave Fly there while he operates to remove the puppies and to find out what has caused the miscarriage.

I go home and wait. My best-loved dog. It's heartbreaking. I can't do or think about anything else. I make tea but I only watch it grow cold. I grab the phone the second it rings. Angus is gentle when he tells me: he had to remove the uterus. I'm nodding my head, thankful that she's alive, before it finally registers. Fly will never breed. I will never have a Fly pup of my own. I'm still trying to digest this when he carries on.

'Could she have been poisoned?'

'Poisoned?' I feel sure I must have misheard him. 'Poisoned? No! Definitely not.'

'It's just that when we took out the ventilator tube it had blood on it. Haemorrhaging in the lungs is usually a sign of poisoning. And there were signs of haemorrhaging everywhere the needle had been.'

I am horrified, but I assure Angus that we use a reputable company, who are incredibly careful, to deal with pest control at Fairspring, and there is never any poison at Fallowlees. I hate the stuff.

I hear him sigh. 'I hate to say this, Emma, but I'm

pretty sure it *was* poison, and that's why she lost the pups.'

I leave Angus to get on with the job of saving my dog. Twenty minutes later he's back on the phone. Fly is fading fast; she has lost too much blood, her gums have gone white. Do I want to leave her, or would I like him to try to save her with a blood transfusion? He adds that the transfusion will be very expensive, and she is already quite far gone. I don't need to think about my answer. I ask him to save her.

The rest of the afternoon passes in a blur. I feel sick. I can hardly even bear to look at my other dogs. They know that something is wrong, and at one point Bill comes inside from his games and lies at my feet while Roy sticks his head on my shoulder and leaves it there. It is so touching it makes me cry. A bit later, when I have still heard nothing, I begin to phone Angus then think better of it. I know he'll call me when there's news.

Eventually I manage to rouse myself. I round up the dogs and we walk to the little lake up the hill behind the farmhouse. It's a picture-book lake, framed by conifers, heather bordering the far shore. I throw a stick on to the smooth dark water for the dogs to fetch and they scramble round the weeds along the shoreline but won't go in any further.

All the while I look obsessively at my phone, terrified that I'm going to miss a call.

Angus doesn't ring until much later when I'm back inside and thinking that I really ought to eat something.

'We've saved her, Emma.' These are his first words. My legs are wobbly and I have to sit down. 'I can't tell you how close it was.'

'Can I come and see her?'

'Of course, whenever you like.'

At the surgery, the nurse tells me more. 'We couldn't find a pulse. I really thought we'd lost her. She's quite a miracle.' She strokes her head. 'She's got a lovely temperament, hasn't she.'

To be honest, I'm slightly surprised to hear this. Though she's gentle with me and people she knows, Fly can often take a dislike to strangers.

Two days later she's home, her wounds held together with staples, her skin covered in bruises. Angus thinks the cause was warfarin used in rat poison, which stops blood from clotting. The slightest touch brings another bruise to the surface. Her belly is black, and so are both of her front legs where the needles for the drips and blood transfusions were inserted. Now she is on a course of vitamin K, which will restore the blood's ability to clot.

I am livid. I've always thought poison is such an indiscriminate way to kill animals however careful one is. I don't know where she picked it up.

When the bill arrives I hardly dare open the envelope. Angus warned me it would be a big one so I can hardly feign surprise. When I finally look at it my heart sinks. Twelve hundred pounds. How the hell am I going to pay that on top of everything else?

Still, I have my dog back. I could never put a price on that.

*　　　*　　　*

Deerplay is a world-renowned hill trial held each June on the slopes of Deerplay Hill in Lancashire. It is limited to seventy-five handlers, each name drawn out of a hat containing a note of every entrant. This year my entry has been successful and

I have travelled down with Roy to give it our best shot, glad to take my mind off money worries for a couple of days.

I had a very early start and thought I might be the first to arrive, but people are already milling about and the barbecue is being fired up for breakfast. It is the first time I have seen the hill. I have marvelled at pictures of it in my sheepdog manuals, but never visited before. It is even more impressive than I thought. The slope starts gradually, but it steepens suddenly. The ground is hard going with deep ditches and rough grasses and rush bushes. A road carves its way up one side of it and the other seems to stretch for miles. The gates are set up already and I can see the line they want the sheep to take. There is a wire pen at the topmost part of the slope from where the sheep will be released. Usually, sheep are kept at the top of a field by shepherds; here, the sheep are too wild to be held by people and so they are contained within the wire until the dog can get up the slope.

I feel nervous already and try to swallow it down. I've got a long way to go before my run at number thirty-eight, and it will do no good to start getting anxious now. Some of the top handlers in the country are here and I've been following the progress of many of them in the farming press. I'm looking forward to this chance to see them in action for myself.

A familiar face comes into view: Chloe Cropper, whose uncle owns this farm. Chloe has been trialling all her life and is a cracking handler. We greet each other and she asks how I'm feeling.

'A bit nervous, to be honest.'

'Don't worry. Our Roys will do it no bother.' Her dog is also called Roy—it is the 'John Smith' of sheepdog names.

We are soon joined by some of the other competitors, old hands at this course, and everyone has a favourite yarn to tell.

'Well, one year a dog went all the way up, jumped the fence and then got hit by a car, jumped the fence back again and carried on to bring the sheep down. Remember that? And another year, do you remember that dog that hit the ditch so hard he ruptured his spleen?'

I must visibly baulk at these tales as Chloe pats my arm. 'Don't listen to them. They love a good horror story. You'll be fine.'

Roy seems unfazed by the whole set-up when I get him out of the car. Typical Roy, he's more interested in weeing on cars and seeing if there are any nice looking trial bitches about.

The first dog goes to the post. I watch as Roy stops sniffing and comes to sit at my feet to see what's going on. The dog sets off at full pelt, curving gracefully up the field, and all is going well until, about halfway up the hill, just as it starts to get steeper, he begins to head in the wrong direction. Instead of following the fence he starts to come in towards the middle of the hill. The handler whistles, but to no avail. The dog crosses his course, which means the handler cannot be placed in the trial. It's all over for them both. He calls his dog off and retires.

'Oh, Roy, I hope that doesn't happen to you.' However, I start to feel much better. The disqualified collie was a good dog and there seems no shame in what happened. I begin to relax and enjoy the day.

After a long wait my turn comes. Oh well, I think, as I make my way to the post, better dogs have messed this up. We are both first-timers and Roy's just a youngster. Roy's head has dropped and he seems to

159

be staring directly at the sheep at the top of the hill, despite the fact they are mere dots to me. 'Away,' I tell him, and off he goes on the perfect line. I have the whistle in my mouth and my hand cupped to my face ready to steer him on to the right path, but I can see that I'll have no problems there as he cruises up the hill and comes in right behind the little packet of woolly Cheviots. And down they come, the small white hill sheep with short legs and a fast run, their tails—kept long for protection against the cold—swinging as they go. They slip perfectly through each set of gates down the hillside and before I know it they are on the level and Roy is in control. Another set of gates neatly met, and then on to the pen. I hold the long rope on the gate as Roy coaxes the sheep inside. It is, of course, a trap, and the wise little creatures know this, but Roy works them close and together we have them boxed in. They back in reluctantly and I slam the gate behind them. I can't help but smile when we come off the field.

I watch the scores for all of the competitors closely throughout the day and at the end I am still in the top twenty, which means I go—along with Chloe—through to a longer and more demanding trial the next day which has two outruns instead of one. At the moment I don't feel nervous, just elated. Good old Roy!

*   *   *

Morning mist clings to the hill like a close-fitting cloak. We can barely see even a few feet in front of us, never mind eight hundred yards up a hill. The competitors huddle around the barbecue, discussing what sort of mist it is and whether it is likely to lift.

160

'It won't be the first time the mist has put paid to it. These hills are notorious.'

We munch bacon sandwiches and sip polystyrene cupfuls of hot bitter coffee, and watch as the mist gradually evaporates and sun breaks through, revealing the hilltops and the letting-out pens on either side of the course.

Game on! The first competitor is called to the post.

The double outrun is one of the toughest tests a sheepdog can undertake. The dog must fetch two packets of sheep from different parts of the course, which tests stamina and intelligence. The dog will also have to demonstrate an ability to listen and to follow commands.

In the hours that follow, a parade of the very best handlers in the country send their dogs round the course, putting on a fantastic display of skill. When it is my turn, I walk to the judge's car and give my name and the dog's name. I look across the first eight-hundred-yard outrun to the letting-out post to see if the sheep are loose yet. The judge squints into the distance then trains a pair of binoculars on them. Yes, he says, they are at the post.

As I walk out, I know people will be watching me, wondering who I am and if my dog is up to it.

'Look,' I say to Roy, and face him in the right direction.

'Come bye,' I tell him and he's off flat out towards the little huddle of dots. It seems to take him forever to get to them as he slows down over the rough ground. I will him on in my head and, thrillingly, he lands right behind the sheep. I whistle a stop command and I have no idea if he takes it because I can no longer see him. I whistle a 'walk on' and I can see the little white dots start to move across the

161

hillside. Gradually they become bigger and bigger until they are finally recognisable as sheep. Roy is right behind them and I leave him to it. He knows where I am and he knows better than I do how his sheep behave.

Finally, he gets them to the post on the level piece of ground. I stop him and shout, 'Look back'. Roy swivels round and turns back up the other hill to gather another three sheep let out to the same starting post we used yesterday. Roy knows his job now, and executes a perfect outrun. We hit all of the obstacles on the way down. With all six sheep united, I now have to drive them through a set of gates on the flat land. I am off-line all the way across but somehow the sheep hit the gates. Next is the pen. I hold the rope for the gate tightly as Roy manoeuvres them close, but before I know it they are past me and round the back. Drat! That's half of my pen points gone now! I gather myself, and the next time Roy edges them closer I am ready: *bang!*—they are in.

The last job is to split off one sheep. This is Roy's forte. As I let the string out, I ask him to cut off the last one. In like a rocket, he takes it away from the bunch, dodging here and there to stop her rejoining the others.

'OK,' shouts the judge. The trial is over. I am so proud of my little black dog. I know we are unlikely to come high in the prizes due to my error at the pen, but I am so pleased with him.

At the end of the day they read out the prize list. To my delight, Chloe and her Roy have won the competition. I am not in the top six but when I go to see the scores later, I discover I was in seventh place.

'Roy, you're an absolute star,' I say, giving him a big cuddle. Being Roy, he looks as if he already knows it.

'I told you our Roys wouldn't let us down,' says Chloe. 'Let's go and celebrate.'

*   *   *

I love Fairspring, I do, but for a while now I have come to feel that my heart is not in it the way it used to be. The long drive to and from work doesn't help, and I'm starting to resent the fact that I've been coming home in the dark to my own farm for all these months. It has started to feel as if Fairspring is preventing me from getting on with my plans for Fallowlees.

But Fairspring pays my wages and the list of expenses is never-ending: I need the pickup fixed, I need to pay for Fly's operation, I need to feed my dogs, pay for petrol, feed *myself*. More and more of my ample driving time is spent worrying about money these days. It is early summer and the countryside is stunningly beautiful, yet I barely register any of its joys. This time last year I would have shared these kinds of worries with Steven. Once again, I feel my solitude and fear I will never find a way out of it. Mum and Dad are always helpful, and I am always asking for their advice; but I don't unburden myself on them. I would hate to sound pathetic or sorry for myself—and, in my head at least, that's how it comes across. I know that if Dad hears even a hint of self-pity, he will only remind me that I chose to stand on my own two feet, I chose Fallowlees and farming and this whole way of life. (I also chose to leave Steven—but he might not say that aloud.) I *do* want this life; but it can be so hard sometimes. This way of life is a daily choice; every new day seems to bring something new to test my resolve.

It is raining again today, which will never help my mood. I park the banana car and go off to get the quad bike. The farm is quiet. Ken and Hilary are away, Archie's got family commitments and it's only when I call Roy and Alfie that I realise with a start that I haven't seen another living soul for three days. It's an unnerving thought.

The wind is howling through the trees, the rain slicing the air horizontally. So much for summer, I think grimly. I am wearing a waterproof coat over my usual weather-beaten jacket, along with the waterproof trousers and wellies that are a staple of my daily uniform. I am wearing a fleecy scarf pulled up over my mouth and nose, which is soaked through by rain on the outside and my hot breath on the inside. Oh yes—ever the glamour puss. I reckon I could teach Kate Moss a thing or two about festival chic.

I'd rather be doing one of the indoor jobs, that's for sure, but when the weather is like this, the need to check the sheep is even more pressing. The fields look empty since all the sheep are huddled right into the lee of trees, walls, anything that might act as a windbreak. They lie with their legs tucked beneath them, their backs to the wind. Raindrops drip rhythmically from the tips of their ears, and every now and then, they shake their lowered heads sending droplets flying.

Quad bikes are a godsend in many ways; I can cover the whole farm in an hour and perform a thorough check. If I were on foot it would take all morning and I could easily miss an ailing sheep tucked away in a corner. However, I am still exposed to everything the elements can throw at me, and the increased wind speed when I accelerate makes for a very miserable job. I just have to get my head down and hunker my body against whatever nature chucks at me. When you are on the move, working up a sweat, farm work during colder weather can be quite a lot more bearable; now, though, it's the bike that's moving, not me. I am static; the dogs are ecstatic—Roy and Alfie seem perfectly happy as they run alongside me with their tongues lolling out, wondering what I'm making such a fuss about. The sheep are looking fed up as only sheep can (imagine Eeyore, with fleece) but they seem healthy and not suffering any ill effects from the atrocious conditions.

As I reach the last field I am starting to think about heading home to Fallowlees, a nice cup of tea next to the Rayburn. It's too wet to do any more farm work today. My mind wanders. The comfy sofa, something tasty to eat, drying-out dogs, a good book would be nice. As I hop off the quad bike and open the gate of the last field, still daydreaming, there is an almighty crash behind me. I whip round to see that a huge bough from a tree just behind the bike has snapped off and hit the ground. The bike had a lucky escape, I think. Good job I didn't park it a few feet further back.

What if I *had* parked a couple of feet further back? What if I'd stayed on the bike a few seconds longer? It would not just be the bike trapped under that enormous bough; I would be, too. I would surely be dead.

I drive through the gate, really quite shaken, unable to stop myself thinking through the possibilities, this near miss I have just had. What if the bough hadn't killed me, but I was left injured, trapped, screaming for help—who would hear me? No one ever comes this way. Ken and Hilary would not be up here for a few days at least. Would Mum realise I was missing—how long would it take for alarm bells to start ringing? I don't always answer my mobile, there'd be no cause for immediate concern there. I might lie there for days and days, the crows would peck out my eyes, then come back for my tongue; foxes and badgers would start to chew on me, other critters too, I would be eaten alive. Someone would find my remains in time, unrecognisable, demolished, a matter for DNA and dental records. The remains of a feast identified in time as poor Emma Gray. That would put me on the map, for sure. Hannah Hauxwell, eat your heart out (pardon the pun).

Blimey, why haven't I thought of any of this before? I've been living in cloud cuckoo land. It would be just as bad if it happened at Fallowlees. Perhaps there'd be a chance of being stumbled on by a forestry worker or a passing hiker but not necessarily. I can go for days there without seeing any sign of human life.

This fallen bough has turned the world into a hostile, dangerous place. Every tree looks a potential killer. I feel remarkably small and vulnerable and—perhaps for the first time since I saw the men in their balaclavas—I realise why the issue of isolation is so very persistent, why everyone is so keen to see me with a man. This is what people have been trying to warn me about. Everyone else sussed it out; everyone apart from me.

I feel a bit calmer when I get home. The rain has stopped. My recovered sheep are grazing contentedly. Bill and Len run around like crazy when I let them out. Bill does a funny little dance around a molehill. Fly is calmer, she's recovering well and wags her tail with pleasure at our arrival.

'Hey, we'll be winning trials together soon,' I tell her. She gives me that goofy smile. 'Bet you can hardly wait, can you, girl?'

A lovely long, hot soak in the bath helps to relax me, but back in bed my mind adopts worry mode again. It is not just what happened earlier. I'm thinking about money again, too, riffing on the familiar theme, 'How Will I Ever Make This Farm Work?' I have a conversation with myself that goes something like this:

DEFENCE	'I have a plan to run the show. The National Trust thought it was good enough. And it could still work.'
PROSECUTION	'Some plan *that's* turned out to be.'
DEFENCE	'And anyway, so what if it goes wrong. I'll just declare myself bankrupt. I'm still young, what does it matter?'
PROSECUTION	'And run back home to Mummy and Daddy? Grow up, Emma. Life is short, there's no time to make mistakes.'

I toss and turn, turn and toss. I switch the pillow this way, that way. This is ridiculous, I need to be up early to be at Fairspring tomorrow and get on with the worming.

What do people usually do when they can't sleep? I don't have any sleeping pills. Relaxation might help, but I can't imagine my brain cooperating. I'm down to counting sheep. I should be able to do it better than most! I start by imagining a green hill peppered with delicate white daisies, and overhead a bright blue sky. A picket fence with a five-bar gate lies halfway up the hill, and little cartoon clouds of sheep come bounding into my picture, taking giant leaps across the fence in the sunshine.

No, no, no! This is all wrong. Surely I can conjure up something a little more realistic. I try again. The scene is the same, but this time the sheep is a Mule, a pretty one with a dark face and alert black ears. She runs up to the fence in an ungainly canter and over she goes. 'One,' I count, as she disappears up and over the hill. Next comes a Blackface with curled horns, a little white snip on her nose and a wild look in her eyes. She gallops in and clears the fence by miles. 'Two.' And now a fat Suffolk with big ears and an enormous girth. She ambles up to the fence but there's no way she can make it over. Instead she sticks her face through the bars in the gate, then, finding herself caught, panics, throws her head up and lifts the gate clean off its hinges. With a shake she frees herself, the gate falls to the ground and she trundles back the way she came.

Suddenly there are sheep everywhere, surging through the opening, coming from all corners of the hill and of my imagination. All breeds, all sizes, all mannerisms, far too many to count, all heading to pastures new. I laugh to myself. Yep, that's more like it!

But counting sheep is not going to get a shepherdess to sleep. I admit defeat and get out of bed and go down to make a cup of tea. Fly and Alfie are in the kitchen—my patients have been allowed to sleep in the house since their illnesses. Fly wags her tail.

168

Alfie, lying on his back on the sofa, his legs in the air, doesn't wake till I fill the kettle.

I take my tea into the porch and open the outside door. The air smells damp and earthy. Midges buzz round my head while moths, attracted by the light, make their ungainly way inside. There is nothing to beat Fallowlees at night. Bats swoop from their nests in the rafters of the sheds. The forest comes alive with noise. Owls hoot, foxes scream. I hear a faint yapping that I can't identify.

I feel as if I'm all alone in a magical world, and in a sense, I am.

I look across to my perfect dog-training field. Somewhere in the damp grass my five Suffolks are snoozing happily. This is where I belong. I feel it so strongly. Devon was a wonderful place, and it has inspired me, but it's not *my* place. This is what I know, and my feeling for this farm is at the very core of my being.

I can make this farm work. I know I can! I want to have it all—the farm, my own sheep, a good job, good dogs. I am being greedy, I know, but someone once told me, 'Reach for the stars and you might hit the ceiling, but reach for the ceiling and you will stay on the floor.'

A thought is beginning to swim into focus. A thought so obvious I can't believe it hasn't occurred to me before.

Tomorrow when I go back to Fairspring I will hand in my notice to Michael.

Chapter Ten

It actually took me a few days to build up the confidence to tell Michael I was leaving, and I hated myself as I told him. He was clearly surprised, which made it even harder. I have learned so much from him. When I made mistakes he never punished me but turned them into a valuable lesson. He was as good a boss as I could ever want. Ever since that starry night, though, my mind had been made up: I knew nothing would sway me. Generous to the last, Michael paid me to continue looking after the ewe lambs on Fallowlees until the autumn when they will go back to Fairspring to be tupped. The eighty lambs are growing like mushrooms, filling out well.

Just as difficult, if not more, was telling Archie, my best friend. He said he understood, and that he was sure it was the right decision for me, but I felt awful all the same. I knew how much I would miss our tea breaks, sitting side by side and sharing our thoughts on dogs and sheep over a scone or piece of Eileen's cake. I knew I'd see him again, but it wouldn't be the same.

*　　　*　　　*

Dave Hyland—or Duracell Dave, as he is commonly known—is the boss of a gang of shearers from New Zealand and has been coming to the UK for the summer shearing for as long as I can remember. He used to turn up at Hawick when I was a little girl, and I have no idea how old he is. I swear he looks no different now from the way he did the first time I saw him. Timeless. He's very strong, and his stamina is legendary, hence the nickname, but he's built like a whippet; I don't think there's a spare bit of flesh on him. He will shear for eight hours straight, drink all night long and start shearing again, none the worse for wear, the next day.

A few days after leaving Fairspring I am working for him as a roustabout or rousie—clearing up and wrapping fleeces—and though I know it'll be a slog, it's too good an offer to turn down now that I don't have a steady income any longer.

At six a.m. I turn up at the shearers' base farm where I am allocated to a team and we head off to a huge farm near the coast, next door to Acklington Prison, to start work at seven. This farm has ten thousand sheep and we expect to shear a thousand of them today. It sounds like a tall order.

My team consists of two Kiwis and one British lad, and it doesn't take long to get to know them. Jason is just nineteen years old, but extremely fast and very talented. He's tall and strong and has a scar down one arm after a childhood incident with a kettle of boiling water.

Nick, who is half Maori, is the joker of the outfit. When he's not shearing, he simply never stops with the patter, and if we're feeling a bit down or getting so exhausted we are about to drop, he'll churn out some jokes to keep our spirits up.

It takes me a while to tune in to the Kiwi accent. When I mishear something Nick says, he stops and looks at me. 'Did you hear about the coach load of tourists in New Zealand? Came across a farm at the side of the road, and the farmer is holding a sheep in a suspicious manner, if you know what I mean. One of the tourists puts his head out the window and says, "Excuse me, sir, but are you shearing?" Farmer growls back at him, "I'm not shearing this sheep with anyone, mate.'"

Nick is a quick shearer, and has an equally quick temper if the sheep don't behave the way he wants them to.

Ed is the opposite of Nick, so laid back he's almost horizontal. He's Northumberland born and bred but has spent such a long time in Australia and New Zealand that in some ways he seems more foreign than the other two. He tells me that when he went to the doctor's for a health check they refused to perform it until he brought his passport in to prove that he was eligible for care on the NHS. Like Nick he works incredibly fast and the pair of them treat their work as a competition to see who gets through the most sheep. And the faster they go, the faster I have to go.

It is a legal requirement to clip or shear the wool from a sheep each year. Once upon a time, the value of all the fleeces would pay the farmers' rent for the year, but such days are long gone and the harsh reality now is that the cost of removing a fleece is sometimes greater than its actual worth.

It is baking hot today and there's no shelter. The sheep, who have been separated from their lambs (who don't need shearing), are channelled up a ramp into the clipping trailer and on to a platform called a race. The clipping trailer is portable, with sliding doors on one side so that the shearer can pull the ewe from the race and on to the boards—the area where the shearing takes place—and which can accommodate three men at a time. My job is to keep the boards clear of fleeces and stray wool. The machines are electric and run off a generator, which has been placed down the field out of earshot. It is noisy enough as it is with three shearers going flat out and the radio blaring.

Since these boys are real professionals, they can shear some of the sheep in less than a minute. Once the wool has been clipped and the sheep has scampered off, I collect each fleece and roll it into a neat bundle that I push into a six-foot by four-foot hessian sheet that hangs in a metal frame in order to accommodate as many fleeces as possible. I regularly have to jump on top of the fleeces so that I can get a few more in. When I am sure that I can't fit another in, I take a needle and stitch the sheet together so that the fleeces are safely packed and ready for sale to the British Wool Marketing Board to be made into carpets and other household items.

Being a rousie might sound like an easy job, but it certainly is not. It is fast and it is furious. As the fleeces come flying at me, I think nostalgically of doing the rounds at Fairspring on the quad bike, cold rain battering my face, even of the long hours and blistered hands of lambing time. I could be there now, overseeing this same operation, instead of being stuck in the middle of it, red as a beetroot and dripping with sweat. The boys are zipping along, sweat dripping off their noses and plopping to the boards, but otherwise unfazed by the heat. I don't think they've even got suncream on, unlike me—I'm lathered in the stuff. Their skin is a deep bronze, but I know I've no hope of ever going that colour.

These sheep are Beulahs, a Welsh breed that clips easily, so the fleeces pile up on the boards at lightning speed. I seem to be on the move all the time trying to keep up with them. Removing the fleece is a skilled operation. Most shearers use a technique called the

Bowen method (after the man who invented it, a New Zealander called Godfrey Bowen). They sit the sheep down between their legs as if it were a sitting dog, and use their non-shearing hand to stretch the skin tightly, thus allowing long, smooth passes of the clippers and producing a superior quality fleece which is continuously falling away from the animal's body, keeping it clean. The clippers are run from a machine above our heads, which operates through a simple cog-turning mechanism that runs the blades together—they're not unlike the clippers you would find in a barber's shop.

Jason, Nick and Ed follow the shearing season round the world. They shear in the UK from May until August, return to Australia and New Zealand for summer there, then the following year it's Europe and back to the UK. It is one continuous routine of long, sheep-filled days and late, booze-filled nights and I honestly don't know how they do it.

The air resounds with the sound of whirring blades, Nick's jokes and music from someone's iPod. I am enjoying it, despite the slog and the inevitable ribbing one expects being the only girl.

'Hey, Emma, you heard the one about the sheep on Viagra?' asks Nick.

'Save that one for tomorrow,' says Jason. 'She might not come back otherwise.'

'What's the nightlife like round here?' asks Nick.

'You think I get time for anything like that? I'm a farmer,' I say as I sew up what I think will be the last but one sack of the day.

'We'll go into the big smoke one night,' says Ed. 'Newcastle on a Saturday night is an eye-opener.' You can tell he's been away a long time as his voice goes up in a question at the end of each sentence just

174

like the Kiwis'.

'I reckon we're almost there.' I'm aching all over. I'm itching all over. I feel as if I'm covered in a layer of grease and I don't dare think what my face looks like. It wouldn't surprise me if my skin was patchy with wool and dead insects like an extra in a horror film.

'Nah,' says Jason. 'We've got another couple hundred to go.'

Two hundred? A sick feeling settles in the pit of my stomach. I'd been counting so carefully. The thought of carrying on for possibly another hour and a half is almost too much to bear.

Nick and Jason are looking at me in a funny way.

'You heard the one about the Pommie who fell for everything?' says Nick.

'Didn't think we'd manage to pull the wool over *your* eyes—'scuse the pun,' says Jason. 'Shoulda seen your face!'

'You bastards!' is all I can manage.

An hour later we're in the pub and I've got an ice cold lager in hand. It's like honey to a bear, blood to a vampire, water in the desert. I have never in my whole life tasted a sweeter liquid.

*　　　*　　　*

We head off to a farm in the Coquet valley, stopping first to buy lunch in Rothbury where there's a renowned baker's. We carry on up the valley. This place is proving to be a real trek. I am at the wheel of the boys' pickup, having quickly assumed the role of driver. It seemed a sensible option—they've always had a skinful the night before.

Ed tries to make a call on his mobile but it won't

work. It really does feel remote out here. We open gates and cross cattle grids and there's still no sign of the farm. We cross fords and bounce along rutted shingle roads that have been partly washed away. I'm starting to doubt that this road goes anywhere, but Ed assures me that he has been here before. The track twists and turns and finally the steading appears within view. The sheep pens are full of Blackfaces. They are my favourite sheep as far as this job is concerned as their fleeces are small and light and I can fit lots into a sheet and not have to spend so much time stitching.

It is a lovely day. Ed has forgotten his iPod, which is a blessing for me since we don't share a taste in music. He is into obscure stuff that hardly even sounds melodic. Instead, we rig up the radio to drown out the machinery's whirr and buzz.

Despite their hangovers, the shearers are soon into the swing of things. The music on the local radio station is much more my thing and I have a little dance and a sing-along as I move between the boards and the packing crate. The morning passes in no time, and it's soon time for lunch. The farmer and his shepherd disappear for theirs and we stretch out on the greasy boards and get stuck into the goodies from the bakery. I let the dogs out and they sniff about and are ready recipients of any crusts we throw for them.

Fly has almost totally recovered from her ordeal. I'm so proud of her. She runs around with the others but constantly looks across to me to see what I'm doing.

'She's devoted to you, that one,' nods Nick in her direction, his mouth full of steak and kidney pie. 'Now if you can find a fella like that, you'll be sorted.'

'Yeah, she's my girl all right. You know, I think if she was human she'd be a wonderful mother and a great cook, she's so maternal.'

'Reminds me of that joke,' says Ed. 'Why do Kiwis marry women? Cos sheep can't cook.'

The New Zealanders of our party are too busy eating to bother responding.

'Yep, she'd do anything for anyone and always put her family first.'

The three men watch me as they chew. Nick rolls his eyes.

I carry on, playing to my audience. 'She'd be deep and dreamy, a quiet type. She'd be one of those people you'd always chat to but never really get to know unless you were a very close friend.'

'Aye, like Dave,' laughs Ed. 'We've always thought he was deep and dreamy, haven't we, lads!'

'Now, those two—' I point a finger at Alfie and Roy, '—they'd be in the army but in very different roles. Roy would be an SAS captain, sharp as they come, he'd look just like Sean Connery in a uniform. He would always have been top of his class during his training, and all his men will look up to him. And he'd be deadly with the women.'

'Just like Dave again,' jokes Jason.

'Alfie would be a private, hardworking and loyal, but he'd probably do something daft like shoot himself in the foot and then end up in hospital keeping the other patients amused with his antics.'

'Wasn't there a crap song about being in the army?' says Ed languidly, taking a swig of Lucozade—their hangover cure of choice.

'I think someone's had too much sun,' says Jason, narrowing his eyes at me.

The music has stopped and a serious voice is

saying something about a special news bulletin. We all sit up and listen. The newsflash is about Raoul Moat, a man whose name I've been hearing for the past couple of days. Recently released from Durham prison, he had gone straight to the home of his former partner where he shot and wounded her, killed her new partner, and the next day seriously wounded a policeman. The police seem to think he is hiding in the Rothbury area and should be considered armed and dangerous. A two-mile exclusion zone has been set up around the village. Nobody is to be allowed in or out.

Rothbury under siege? What a bizarre thought. *Nothing* ever happens in Rothbury. It's a small market town, a quiet place to live, a base for walkers and other such mild and responsible and peaceful types. We're lying up here on this remote hillside amid a pile of sheep's wool and some very naked sheep, and the eyes of the world are on a place a few miles down the road. It feels unreal.

We all look at each other. A murderer running loose in Rothbury.

'It's like an episode of *Midsomer Murders*!' I say to the gang, just as the farmer and shepherd come back to tell us all about it, having just seen it on TV.

'Aye, it was on the BBC and all,' says the shepherd, almost proudly.

'I reckon he's in the woods,' says the farmer. 'Plenty of good places to hide round here.' He looks at me sternly. 'I wouldn't go home if I were you, lass.' He knows that as the crow flies I'm only half a dozen miles through the forest from Rothbury. I am both frightened and exhilarated at the same time.

The rest of the day seems to drag by. The parade of sheep is monotonous, and the shearers seem to

178

be shearing unbearably slowly. Every time I hear the news come on I strain to hear the latest development, but the machines drown out the detail and I can't afford to get behind with my work.

At one point I'm sure I hear that armed police and dogs are searching Harwood Forest, and I can't help but think that it would be a good place to hide. My sheep certainly thought so, but I may have misheard. Mum and Dad will be desperately trying to get in touch but I'm cut off from the rest of the world until we get out of the valley.

We are stopped by the police on the way home, right on the outskirts of Rothbury. They want to know our names and where we've been, whether we've seen anything. We have to get out of the pickup so that they can inspect it properly. I put on my serious face but I am feeling quite excited really; how strange it is that with this murderer on the loose I am prickling with the thrill of fear, yet faced with everyday dangers of farm life and isolation, I can spiral into real panic.

As I drop the boys off at their base, my mobile rings and I prepare to speak to Mum but instead it's Anna from the National Trust, wondering if I've heard the news.

'I don't think you should go back to Fallowlees tonight,' she says. 'Just as a precaution.'

I thank her for her concern, but I don't promise anything. I've got animals to see to, dogs to feed. I know I'm going home whatever. Besides, what interest does this man have in me? He's said that he won't hurt anyone. If he wants food he can have it. I joke to Anna that I'll leave him a hot meal on the doorstep and hope that keeps him happy—if it doesn't drive him away—but I don't think she's amused.

179

I'm desperate for a shower when I get home, but first I just stand and look out over Fallowlees. It never looks more beautiful than it does on these long summer evenings, when night barely gets a chance to dampen down the fields and the forest in darkness before the sun appears again over the coast. In this shimmering light, Greenleighton Moor reminds me of a desert.

When everything is so picture-perfect, so tranquil, it's quite impossible to add a murderer into the scene. My Suffolks graze as if they are painted on to the landscape. The dogs bark a welcome home. All the same, I perform a quick check of the house. Nothing has been disturbed. No fugitive under the bed, or sitting at my table feasting on my leftovers—heaven help him.

After I've eaten I'm in the front field checking on the sheep when I hear what sounds like a helicopter in the distance. The noise gets louder until it appears over the treetops and carries on until it is hovering just above my head. The grass quivers all around, my hair blows madly round my face. Then, perhaps having ascertained that I don't match the description of a thirty-seven-year-old male fugitive, the beast does an about turn and shoots off and away.

I decide to leave the front door unlocked that night. My logic being that if this man does come hunting for food, he can come in and take it without terrifying me by hammering my door down or climbing in through my window. Nevertheless, I lie awake for longer than usual in bed, alert to every little noise.

'Go to sleep,' I tell myself. 'I'm not counting any more flipping sheep—I've had enough with their fleeces.' And soon after, I drift off.

Every night I follow the same routine. I'm not scared, I tell myself, but I go through all the rooms and check the outbuildings, just in case. Before I leave for work in the morning I do the same. Whatever would happen if I actually found Raoul Moat in one of my sheds, snoozing in a corner, or, even worse, sitting there looking at me, I have not quite figured out. But I perform my checks anyway.

Today, on my way out, a police van is parked outside Redpath. They have already checked the old farmhouse, but it looks as if they are going through it again. At the bottom of the track I am stopped, as always, and the police check the boot of banana car before they let me go. Once I made the mistake of telling them I had my dogs to look after me, and they just laughed. As Bill and Roy had made friends within about thirty seconds with the pair who stopped by Fallowlees one evening, I knew I was fooling myself if I thought they were going to frighten any intruders away.

Today we are shearing at High Towers. It is a Sunday and since the boys were on the drink yet again last night—in a full-on Saturday way—they are feeling sorry for themselves. When I pick them up they are armed with bottles of Lucozade and wearing scowly expressions. Ed is OK, as he was the designated driver for the evening, but Jason and Nick look downright ill. 'A bit crook,' as they tell me. Ed and I share a smug smile.

Somehow I manage to get completely lost; each road looks just like the last. Jason is groaning and complaining in the back and when I glance at him and Nick in the rear view mirror they both look

181

distinctly grey about the gills. Tensions heighten as everyone gets more and more frustrated. I shoot past a turning I should have taken. Jason shouts for me to stop. I slow down and the pickup is still moving as he leaps out, vomiting violently at the side of the road. Nick and Ed jeer from the car. 'Yer soft cock, Jase!'

'Don't be so rotten,' I say to them, but they don't care.

After a bout of prolonged retching, Jason gets back in.

He smiles. 'Aye, I feel much better now.'

'Well you smell a lot worse,' says Ed, sniffing the air.

'Ugh!' yells Nick. 'You dirty bugger, you've sicked on your boots.'

Ed and I turn round, and sure enough, there is a peculiar-looking orange substance on them.

We all screech and jump out the car and Jason wipes his feet on the grass verge.

'It's only Lucozade, you drongo.'

'Yeah, right, bro. Didn't look like Lucozade to me.'

Back in the car I take a quick look at my directions and decide I know where I'm going now. I try to do a U-turn, but that's no mean feat considering the length of the shearing trailer. The boys are particularly unhelpful.

'Right hand down, no, your other right . . . I mean up . . . no, down . . .'

I've been going backwards and forwards for a while now, and even ended up in the hedge a couple of times, when up rocks a police car. That shuts the boys up since they stink of booze. I'm sure the trailer is heavier than the legal weight I am allowed to tow.

'Shit!' I say under my breath. I've no doubt the police could find something to pull us up for, whether the size of the trailer, or my poor—and probably illegal—execution of a U-turn in the middle of the road, or even the status of my foreign occupants. I manage to turn the darn thing round at last, with no more quips from my passengers. The police car watches and waits. As I drive past the panda car, I acknowledge their patience with a wave and a nod, then I watch in my mirror as I carry on back down the road we'd come along before making the turning to the farm. They're not following us. We all breathe a sigh of relief.

'Phew,' says Nick. 'Must be looking for old Moaty. Got bigger fish to fry than a dirty old shearer set-up.'

The farmer comes to greet us as we unload. He's a typical old-school type, my favourite kind. He has hands like shovels, a week's worth of stubble on his face, and he must be in his mid-sixties. His face is weathered, and the wrinkles around his mouth and eyes give the impression he's always smiling. Despite the fact we are half an hour late he is cheerful and brushes off my apology.

'Don't worry, lass, there's no panic. We've got all day.'

We banter on for a while about the weather, the price of lambs and of course the latest topic of conversation round these parts, Raoul Moat, while the boys set the trailer up.

'You'll be wanting a cup of coffee before you start,' he says, and the boys' faces light up.

'Aye, I'll take that as a yes, then,' and he disappears into the farmhouse and shouts for his wife to fetch us some drinks.

We sit on the greasy shearing boards, sipping the scalding coffees. Today is going to be a relaxed affair, I can tell, and I'm thankful for it since our last job was not so friendly. We were not welcomed; just dismissed to get on with it. Farmers like our host today are a dying breed now that farming is becoming more industrialised and employs fewer people. Those newer farms are slick operations, controlled by spreadsheets, gross margins and computers. It's a sad fact and while I munch on a giant slice of the farmer's wife's homemade millionaire's shortbread I think back on my farming childhood and some of the great characters I've met over the years. People like Archie. I wonder how many younger Archies there are out there.

The sheep are in good nick and the shearers fly through them—and yet I'm never overwhelmed as the farmer has enlisted the help of some of his family. Whenever I feel that I'm getting behind, someone will be there to take the strain off me and wrap a few fleeces while I do the stitching.

At bang on twelve o'clock, the universal lunchtime for farmers, we are invited into the house. Massive oak beams support lofty ceilings; an Aga twice the size of my Rayburn takes up most of one side of the kitchen; ornamental mugs hang on hooks that at one time would have boasted drying hams. The room is cluttered with household and family items, yet it's also spotless. Pictures of children and grandchildren peer out from frames everywhere, interspersed with the odd one of a favourite sheepdog or a prize-winning sheep.

The farmer's wife is as welcoming as her husband, and points us towards the large enamel sink to wash the grease off while she busies herself with the next round of teas and coffees. A vast bowl of fresh salad sits on the table. Beside it is a warm quiche, full of bacon and cheese, while some creamy homemade coleslaw is the most inviting I've ever seen. We start with a bowl of potato and leek soup, and there is bread straight from the oven to clean our dishes with. The boys are unusually quiet.

'Leave room for your pudding, won't you,' says our hostess as we tuck into the next course. The boys and I exchange glances, wondering how on earth we are going to fit in anything else. Perhaps I shouldn't have taken quite so much coleslaw. But how can we decline when she's gone to so much trouble? Then she fetches out the rhubarb crumble, made, she tells us, with rhubarb fresh from the garden, and we find ourselves wolfing down a bowlful each loaded with custard.

I can feel the waistband of my jeans digging in. Jase looks miles better now, the hangover a mere memory.

'What a feed!' he says, and everyone laughs.

The subject turns to the ongoing Raoul Moat saga.

'You not worried out there all by yourself?' the farmer asks me when I tell him where I live.

'Nah, I reckon he'll not bother walking all that way, and if he tries the midges'll get him first.'

'Or the adders,' says Nick. 'I hear there's some particularly big ones hang around your place. Of course they prefer tasty young sheilas, but if they get the chance of Moaty, too, well, they'll think their boat is in.'

'Your place sounds like it'd be a good stake-out,' says Jason. 'Now, if I was a murderer on the run in Rothbury, I'd be heading right your way. Nice big farmhouse in the middle of nowhere, views for miles around, a nubile maiden like yourself to hold hostage . . .'

'Shurrup, Jase,' says Ed. 'Stop winding her up.'

185

'It's all right. It really doesn't bother me,' I say. And it's true. I'm rather enjoying the drama of living on the doorstep of a place that's found itself in the national news. Perhaps I'm a little more jumpy when I'm at home, but that's all. To be honest, I think it's pretty unlikely that Moat is still in Rothbury, if he's ever been there.

'I bet he's long gone,' I say. 'No way could he be hiding in a place that size with all those police about.'

'Don't be so sure,' Nick pipes up. 'Some journalist reckons she saw him walking down the high street yesterday.'

'Someone else thinks he broke into his greenhouse and ate all his tomatoes.'

'Yeah, I heard that one,' says Ed. 'And some old biddy reckons he raided her fridge.'

'Well, he won't find much in mine apart from some old milk and dog vaccines,' I laugh. 'Don't think that would sustain him through a stand-off.'

'He'll go barking mad first,' says someone, to our groans.

Back in the shearing shed we make a sluggish start to our afternoon's labours, not used to such good lunchtime fare. The farmer assures us we'll be done by four, but I'm not so sure. I can barely summon up the energy to clamber into the sheet to stamp the fleeces down. The farmer has no such problems—perhaps he is used to a big midday meal, or perhaps he was just more restrained than we were. I feel a bit embarrassed. We must have looked like vultures descending on it all, accustomed as we are to the lunchtime delights of crisps and sandwiches. I'm not sure the boys eat much better in the evening—from the sound of their conversations, I sometimes think they exist on beer and cigarettes.

With everyone pitching in, we make a good finish and stop at the pub on the way home. I can't imagine we're very popular walking into the bar, smelling as we do of grease and sheep shit and sweat, but this is a country pub and used to being frequented by farmers, albeit slightly more respectable ones than us. We order a pint of lager each and take them outside into the sunshine. I always thought girls who drank pints were, well, *not nice girls* as my Mum would say; but this job has changed me. What do I care what someone thinks of me? I am as dirty as these strapping men are. In fact, at first glance I could probably be mistaken for one of them.

*   *   *

For a lot of the lads, shearing in the UK is a sort of holiday—they work hard but they also want to see the country and to have a good time while they're here. Many of them spend as much as they earn, and considering that the quickest shearers can earn more than four hundred pounds on a good day that's a decent wad of spending money. Tonight Duracell Dave has organised a night out for his lads in Newcastle, and I've been invited too. I put on a short skirt, summery top and the customary warpaint, then head off to meet them in a local town from where we'll head into Newcastle together.

Up until now I haven't seen any of the boys in anything other than the shearer's uniform of tight, double skinned trousers—a bit like skinny jeans—and a long wife-beater vest that drops to mid-thigh so that their backs are protected from the elements when they are bent over. But who are these smartly coiffed specimens waiting for me? And is that *really* aftershave I can smell?

I recognise Dave first, Dave the never-aging, in a checked shirt and clean trousers. Nick is similarly dressed in smart jeans with his hair gelled, and Jason, the youngster of the group, looks quite at ease in a trendy looking outfit. But the biggest surprise is Ed, who has had a haircut and a shave (the first in weeks, I reckon), which to my astonishment reveals that he is quite the looker!

As I step out of the car, I am greeted with a series of wolf whistles. I suppose I've undergone quite a radical change, too, since they last saw me. Dave is the first to speak. 'That's a bit revealing,' he says, looking me up and down. I can see he's playing the fatherly role tonight, keen to protect me from the boys, or whatever lurks in the streets of the big city.

'Come on, Dave, you've been into Newcastle before. You know how dowdy I'm going to look compared to most of the girls out tonight. No one's going to give me a second glance once we're there.'

He tuts under his breath and sighs. I think he knows I'm right.

I'm in the mood to party. It feels great being dressed up for a change, to be rid of the dirt and the grease, and I'm determined to enjoy myself.

The taxi drops us at the Bigg Market, the focus of the city's nightlife. It is heaving. It's a cool night and I'm feeling a bit chilly, but one of the first girls we see walks past us wearing a bikini. Nick, who's the only one of the party never to have experienced the delights of a Saturday night in Newcastle, stares after her as she sashays past, and the others aren't much better. She might be the most extreme example of Newcastle dress-code on party night, but to be honest no one is wearing much more. It's a sea of tiny skirts or shorts and bits of string pretending to be tops. I have never seen so much bare flesh on display so far from a sunny beachside. Size is no matter—the overweight are stuffed into their outfits, ripples of spray-tanned flesh oozing out in all directions. I feel very demure.

Nick shakes his head. 'Emma, what's wrong with you? You're wearing far too many clothes for this place.'

We dodge the people handing out flyers for nightclubs and manage to find somewhere to sit in a crowded pub, where the talk keeps returning to shearing. We might talk about Raoul Moat, Newcastle pubs or north-eastern weather, but before we know it we're talking sheep again. You'd think we would want a change of subject, but no; sheep are these boys' life. There is nothing else they really want to talk about. And I suppose I've got a bit of a one-track mind, too, so it's no hardship.

None of them makes a pass at me—nor do I push things in that direction. We're so used to each other now, and I think they see me as one of them which, secretly, I take as a compliment.

*   *   *

Even though I have been with them for a few weeks now, I still find it fascinating to watch the shearers in action. They work so deftly, so methodically, each stroke uncovering more and more of the sheep underneath. They use a constant rocking motion that settles the sheep as they move around her, never stopping or slowing down. They are silent throughout most of the operation other than to shout for me to spray an odd nick or cut that can happen if the sheep decides to kick or struggle. Then it is my job as rousie to rush over with a treatment of antiseptic and fly repellent. Thankfully that doesn't happen often.

The new growth on a sheep is called the 'rise', and the boys' jobs are made easier if the rise is evident. A rise is a sign of a happy, healthy sheep, one that has had a good dose of sunshine throughout the year, but it might be absent if a ewe has been ill, or if she is older, or if she has been working hard feeding three lambs. Sheep like this make the shearers' job much harder since their fleece is often welded to its wearer, and the ewe is more likely to kick out during the long drawn-out process of removing it. The shearers can be heard to mutter all manner of filth under their breath when the going gets tough, and I have certainly learned a small book's worth of new swear words with these boys. The only person who never utters a word during shearing is Ed, and nor do I ever see him lose his temper. He works calmly and quietly, and his manner seems to rub off on the sheep too.

Today we are in a shed, for which I say a silent prayer of thanks. At least in a shed you can regulate your own body temperature, put on and take off clothes as you require. I seem to be permanently boiling or freezing when we're outside. The shed is huge and chock-a-block with sheep. I look at them all, aware that by the end of the day I will have picked up and wrapped up every bit of wool before my eyes. I ask Matt, the shepherd here, how many there are and he replies that there's about nine hundred—a fairly standard number for us. I can't really complain since I am paid per fleece, and with my team being so quick I am earning far more than the girls who were allocated slower teams to work with. All the same, the sight of so many of them in one place fills me with weariness. Ed sees my expression.

'Best not to, you know. Never look at them or count them, just keep your head down and keep going.' He knows what he's talking about: he was in the papers in Australia for shearing solidly for sixty days without a day off. I smile and shrug, and lend a hand setting up the trailer. The machines need to be lifted up, the race set up, and I need to line my packing crates with sheets. Before I know it, we're off again. The fleeces come thick and fast and I am soon down to a T-shirt and sweating in a most unattractive way.

Ed is clipping a particularly skinny sheep and is nearly finished when I hear him say, 'There you go, sweetheart,' and see him lowering its inert mass off the boards. I go over to see what's up and Ed is standing on the trailer looking over her. She is stretched out, limp and lifeless. It sometimes happens that sheep die during the shearing process, perhaps the result of a heart attack, or in this case, simply not being able to cope with the stress of being sheared. She's very lean, her hip bones protruding, and her eyes have a dullness to them. I crouch over her and tap the skin by the tear duct. She blinks, barely, but it's definitely a blink.

'She's a goner, Emma,' says Ed with a shake of his head. 'I would just drag her out the way.'

I move her to the side as the boys carry on working. Jason and Nick haven't even stopped. But after every few fleeces I go over to have a look at the skinny girl. She's coming round, and bit by bit I can see the life flowing back into her body. She's weak, but I manage to sit her on her chest, propped up with some rolled-up fleeces I place by her shoulders. By the time we stop for lunch she's sitting unassisted on her chest.

I let the dogs out while the boys light up for their 'smoko'—as they call their break—then come back to fuss over the poor creature.

Nick draws on his roll-up. 'Emma, she's not your problem. Leave her to the farmer.'

'I know, but I feel sorry for her.' I carry across a bucket of water and she sucks on it furiously.

Ed wanders over and raises an eyebrow. 'You know, I think she might just make it.' And I smile, because I think he's right. By the end of lunch she's standing on wobbly legs and goes off to join the rest of the shorn ewes.

Nick looks on. 'Well, I suppose you were right. There's life in the old girl yet.'

I feel as if I'm drowning in fleeces this afternoon, but I still cast an eye every so often towards the ewe. She looks brighter all the time. Neither the farmer nor the shepherd have been witness to her near demise, so they pay her no attention, and I know that the shearers really aren't worried—they do this for the money, and though they take pride in their work, they have little concern for the welfare of any individual creature. But I watch the ewe as she's jostled out of the shed with the rest of the batch to join the lambs in the field, and I feel happy to think that she'll live another day. Although she's still hanging to the back, she's keeping up with the others. The farmer won't notice.

I'm not cut out for this, I think. Wrapping fleeces is all right for a season to earn some cash, but it's too much like a factory line for me. I know that this can never be my future. I need something with heart and soul to thrive.

Chapter Eleven

My eyes are closed. It is dead of night. Yet I can sense car headlights flash across my room. It must be pulling up in my yard. I daren't open my eyes. Who would turn up at this time? I listen carefully. The car stops, I hear a door open and close, the sound of careful footsteps on the gravel and, to my horror, the creak of my front door opening and then closing again with its gentle click. I cannot move. Where could I go anyway? The front door is the only door in the house. Someone is climbing up the stairs, one step at a time. My heart is beating so hard. My bedroom door opens. I know I should run but I couldn't move a limb if I wanted to. Terror clutches my chest as I sense someone creeping towards my bed. I open my mouth to scream and no noise comes out.

I awake with a start. I'm shaking. It takes me a while before I realise it was only a dream, a terrible dream. I am still scared, though, and my first instinct is to go out to the kennels and bring the dogs indoors to keep me company. I cannot face the dark by myself, not after that nightmare. Instead I turn on the light and read a book until dawn breaks, when, more relieved than I can say, I get up and go down to greet them.

We stride out together towards the forest, and as they gambol around enjoying the unexpectedly early start, I wonder what I was so worried about.

'I'm such a silly thing,' I say to them. 'What's there to worry about round here? And with you lot to look after me, eh?'

Sunlight has begun to streak the sky as a new day

develops before our eyes. As we get close to Redpath, a deer raises its startled head at our approach. A young fawn stands nearby and the doe calls a warning to it. The pair pause for a moment and look towards us before jumping off through the long grass and over the fence, back into the safety of the trees. But as the adult turns I see a mark on her rump next to her pretty white tail, a square patch devoid of hair.

'Hello, old girl, remember me?' I say to her departing behind. The deer I hit all those months ago made it through and, even better, she has given birth.

'I bet *they* didn't have to worry about old Raoul Moat,' I say to the dogs, who look unconcerned and disappear after a rabbit. 'And you lot the same, eh? You don't know you're born.'

Raoul Moat had evaded capture for seven days, until finally killing himself during a stand-off with armed police. I wonder if the dream was a sign that I was more worried than I cared to admit about the situation. The seeming reality of it has unnerved me. I've never had such a chilling, lifelike dream before. Perhaps my blasé attitude to living on my own is just a mask to disguise a deep-rooted fear.

I think about that dream for days.

*　　　*　　　*

I've finished shearing now, and though we all had a good laugh together, I'm relieved. The boys are moving on. I wonder if I'll see them next year.

A while ago I booked myself up to do sheepdog displays at a public farm called Whitehouse, on the edge of Morpeth, but I've had another idea gnawing away at me, too, and I decide it's time to put it into action. For a long time I have been scanning the poultry section in the small ads, and today I finally see what I want: Indian Runner ducks for sale.

I arrive on a rundown council estate in Sunderland with grey pebble-dashed houses built side by side, row upon row. The street is heaving with life; kids in hoodies ride their bikes along the pavement, women pushing prams natter on street corners. Two hard-looking dogs in leather harnesses, each walked by an equally hard-looking owner, stop to sniff each other. It's a far cry from Fallowlees.

I check the house number on the scrap of paper in my hand. I'm at the right place, which is nothing short of a miracle since the primitive satnav on my phone stopped speaking to me long ago. I knock on the door and a skinny lad of about sixteen opens it. I ask for Dean and tell him I've come about the ducks. He invites me to come through.

The inside of the house is something else. Hutches containing all manner of creatures lined up in tiers along the hallway. A few guinea pigs chuckle at me as I pass by and a large lop-eared rabbit sits glaring through the bars of its cage. There is sawdust and hay all over the floor. I make my way through the living room and get a glimpse of some day-old chicks under a heat lamp next to the fireplace. A great big Staffordshire dog says hello by sticking his nose in my crotch. I push him away and follow the lad out the back to the garage.

'They're in here,' he says. 'They make too much mess to stay in the house.'

Under the heat lamp are eight, perfect, day-old chocolate Runner ducklings. I challenge anyone not to melt into a puddle at the sight of such mini-cuteness—covered in fluffy-fluffy down, and the sweetest chirruping sound cheeping from their teeny-tiny beaks.

The lad points to the other end of the garage. 'Those are the adults.'

They are a mix of colours, mainly black, white and brown, but one has the petrol green tinge of a wild mallard on his neck. They are not pure Runners but they are as good as. They make a scruffy-looking bunch, but endearing none the less. They stand bolt upright, like penguins.

'I'll take them all,' I say.

The lad tells me about his love for animals and how one day he'd like a little farm of his own and it's good to know that dreams like that can flourish even in such unlikely settings as this. It's the same for farming as for any other way of life—youngsters are always willing, always capable, always alert for new opportunity; they just need the right guidance, someone to encourage them, and a few breaks to get them on their way and keep them there.

We load the ducks into my yellow car—which, with its boy racer looks, seems to fit right in. In fact, a small crowd gathers as we bring out first the adults and then the box of little ducklings. I wave goodbye and I'm sure that old banana wheels gets one or two admiring glances as we growl our way out of the street.

*   *   *

I've been working hard all year so that Roy has enough points to compete in the English National Sheepdog Trials. I took him for an eye test. The last dog I took for an eye exam was Fly, who had failed the test. At the time, I was devastated and that experience certainly made me more nervous this time around. I should not have worried. The specialist gave Roy's peepers a clean bill of health.

I took Alfie with me, too, figuring that I might as well have him tested at the same time even though I knew he wouldn't have enough points to enter this year's competition. The vet fell silent during the examination, peering into his eyes with great intensity.

I gulped. Oh, please, no more problems. When the vet straightened up he asked me if Alfie had suffered badly from worms as a youngster. I told him that he was quite wormy when I got him as an eleven-week-old pup. He nodded his head. Alfie had a few holes in his eyes from the worms, he said, but there was nothing too much to worry about, it was just better that I should know.

There are four national trials held each year, in England, Ireland, Scotland and Wales, during the months of July and August. The top one hundred and fifty dogs in each country compete for one of fifteen places to go to the International. But getting to national level is hard enough as the points threshold is so high. Roy has fourteen points, earned through placings in open trials throughout the year. I sent off his certificate and the list of his points and sat back to hear if they were enough to win us through.

The day I got home to find the letter from the sheepdog society in the porch was like hearing about Fallowlees all over again. I couldn't believe we had made it. Roy and I were in the national trials, and due to run at the end of the first day. This year the competition was to take place in Alnwick, not far away. I take it as a good omen.

When the day comes, I am so nervous and excited

197

I wake up an hour before my alarm goes off and decide to get up, giving up on the idea of catching any more sleep. After walking the dogs I put all but Roy back into their kennels and take Roy up for a run on the Mules in the front field. He's in fine fettle this morning, confident and powerful. I practise a few sheds with him, splitting them in half and in half again until I have only one sheep left, then getting him to hold the single one. It's all good practice for later in the day.

At eight o'clock the first dog is about to run. Nearly every sheepdog enthusiast in England is here today and I am proud to think that they are in my home county, Alnwick Castle, home to the Duke of Northumberland, being the event's spectacular backdrop. The field is long and wide, with ever such a slight uphill slope. The outrun will be at least four hundred yards. The pen is there and a ring to shed the sheep in is marked out with piles of sawdust.

Mum and Dad have travelled down from Hawick to watch me. It will be the first time they have ever seen me in an open competition and I am nervous to show them that I am up to it, especially since I am always banging on to them about how busy the dogs and I are with our trials at the weekends and how well they are all shaping up. Grandma and Granddad, Mum's parents, who live in nearby Alnmouth, have also come to see me run, as well as my Uncle Toffa who has brought Granny, Grandpa Len's widow, and some of my cousins. And Aunty Lynne has come straight from having a scan for her third baby.

Each run is allowed fifteen minutes and today there are fifty dogs competing. I do a quick spot of maths and realise that by the time Roy and I run, the light could be getting poor. However, there's no point getting worked up about it now. I decide to enjoy the day with my family and wait until it's my turn.

The sheep are proving to be quite flighty and are liable to take off if the dog is too tough on them; they also appear to have an aversion to the first set of gates. It's all providing me with useful information for when it's me up there. I picture which direction the sheep will go, where Roy should be, and how to handle them. Despite their flightiness, they are still manageable and some good high scores are coming out.

I look at Roy who has been watching the proceedings with interest, punctuated, in typical Roy fashion, with a bit of flirting. Well, I can't blame him really with all these talented bitches floating about, giving him the eye.

By five o'clock I begin to get antsy, despite the fact there are still plenty of runs to go. I get the impression that my grandparents are getting a bit bored. It's a long day for them, and it's hard to be interested in every run when you don't know the competitors. They must all blur into one. The light is just starting to fade when an announcement comes over the tannoy that runs forty-four to fifty will instead take place the following morning. Roy and I are number forty-four.

'I'm so sorry, Emma,' says Mum, 'but there's just no way we can come back tomorrow.' Grandma and Granddad are shaking their heads sadly, too. My heart sinks. I have been looking forward to my family seeing me run so much that I ask the course director, Mike, if there's a chance that I could run today. He says it's up to me, and that I can make my mind up after the preceding three runs have been completed.

I'm pretty adamant. 'My family are all here to watch, and I've been psyched up all day for this. I don't think I can face another sleepless night!'

'Well, don't commit yourself just yet,' says Mike. 'Keep an open mind.'

The next dog on the field has an absolutely cracking run; the sheep are quiet and settled, it's one of the best runs of the day. In my head I am weighing up the pros and cons of running tonight. Richard Montgomery, a talented triallist, once won the national in fading light as the last run of the day. It might just work for me, too. The tricky sheep seem to be so much mellower now. I watch the next run and this time the sheep aren't quite so settled but the dog is pushing them hard so it's not really possible to tell if it's him or the dwindling light that is affecting them. The duskiness is certainly making the obstacles harder to judge. As the forty-third dog goes to the post I am still questioning myself. If this run takes the full fifteen minutes allocated, then it will certainly be too dark for me to run. Roy, alert at the end of my lead, seems unbothered either way. I feel myself relax a little. He is a relaxed easy-going type of dog and so far my nerves have never transmitted themselves to him but his chilled-out attitude does tend to work its magic on me.

I haven't been paying attention. Mum calls to me: the last run has been disqualified! It seems that the sheep had been difficult around the post and the dog tried to stop them breaking away with a bite. Now's the time to decide—run now in front of my family or come back on my own tomorrow? The crowd has dissipated slightly which fuels my confidence; but then again, the last two rounds diminished my confidence levels to barely there. In the end it's my family who make the difference between yes and no: I tell Mike I'm ready to run.

'You sure about that?'

'Yeah, I think so.'

'Well, good luck.'

He opens the gate to the field. I release Roy from the lead he has been tethered with all day and he runs ahead to stand at the post waiting for me. The tannoy announces me: Emma Gray from Northumberland and her dog Roy, who is three years old, in their first national.

I walk to the post to join Roy. The sheep are at the far end of the course. They look a bit hazy in the gloom and already I doubt my decision.

'Away!' I tell Roy, and he is off on a good line to the five white-faced creatures four hundred yards away. I can hardly make him out as he closes in behind the little packet. But as he comes to the point of balance he doesn't give the sheep as much room as they need, they see him too suddenly and take flight, setting off diagonally across the field at full speed and in completely the wrong direction. I whistle fast and hard to Roy and he shoots off to try to outrun them and turn them on to the right track. Further and further the sheep get before Roy is finally ahead of them and able to turn them back and steer them towards the first set of gates. These are the gates that have been giving people trouble all day and there has been plenty of speculation as to why, whether it's the shadows they cast or perhaps the fact that the sheep have been kept in a field with cattle grids and aren't used to gates. Somehow Roy successfully forces them through. The pesky creatures bolt yet again. Roy has to work very hard to hold them together and as they come close to me to make the turn around the post they stop and start to threaten him. I can feel despair starting to build inside me. This is not how I imagined my first national would be. Where is the smooth, controlled run I know Roy is capable of? What about all the glory and pride?

As Roy fights them round my feet they take off on the first leg of the drive and there is nothing Roy can do to steer them through the gate. He turns the speeding sheep towards the next set of gates but I cannot judge them at all. I whistle Roy on to what I think is the right line but they gallop right past and with them go my hopes for my little black sheepdog. I know I have dropped below standard after missing two gates and I turn to the judge's box and signal my retirement. Mike shakes his head and urges me to continue but the sheep have already taken off towards the exhaust pen. I call for Roy and he comes over looking pleased with himself, his long tongue hanging out, his mouth wide open drinking in the air. He loves his work so much.

I walk off the field. Mike comes over and puts a hand on my shoulder.

'You OK?'

'Yes. Never mind.' I'm trying to put on a brave face but I'm devastated, and worse is to come. I have to face my family now: Mum, Dad, Grandma, Granddad, Granny, my cousins and my uncle.

I can tell they don't know what to say.

I shrug, 'Oh well.'

'Never mind,' says Granddad. 'It was dark, you couldn't help it.'

Dad puts an arm round me and gives me a squeeze. 'Don't worry. You got here—now that's an achievement in itself. I'm proud of you for that.'

'Yes,' echoes Mum. 'And it's just your first time.'

It doesn't matter how kind everyone is to me, I feel horribly disappointed. It's even worse when I look at Roy. He is such a capable dog and I feel I have let him down. He understands sheep better than I ever could. If he were the pilot and not me, things would have been different. I kneel down and give him a cuddle and he responds by licking my face. Luckily he doesn't care. He's had a good day out and enjoyed the sausage from the burger stand. And we'll try again.

*   *   *

Fallowlees grows weeds. Many of them are beautiful, but they are still weeds. I've got three varieties of thistle alone. One is small and very spiny with bright green leaves and a small flower. Another is more like a bush with large dark leaves and long dangerous spines. But the most beautiful is the elegant boar thistle, which has deep purple flowers—though I have come across an albino one. These thistles are taller than I am, their main stem the girth of my arm.

Foxgloves are also abundant, happy as they are to grow in the shade or recently cleared woodland, while my meadow is a veritable bouquet of rushes, buttercups, and clover.

However, none of this is good for livestock, or indeed for any kind of production, and I have had to buy a sprayer to keep the weeds in check. The sprayer fits on the back of my quad bike with a long lance and allows me to target the thistles and nettles without killing the meadow grasses and flowers.

I know it is a long-term investment, but it is still money I would rather not have spent. I look at the pickup. Yet again. Replacing the engine just keeps being put off and put off with each new demand on my funds. The generator is like a diesel-guzzling dragon, always crying for nourishment; the Rayburn is almost as bad. Then there's the cost of petrol these days—not an area in which I can really make any savings. And I still haven't paid the vet's bill . . . It's on my mind most of the time, and if I do manage to forget it for a while, later that day there'll be a message on my voicemail reminding me that it is still outstanding.

The long and the short of it is that I can't afford it. It's all getting on top of me. My rent on the farm is due, too. I feel stressed, frustrated and emotional all the time.

I go to a local trial with Roy and Alfie one Saturday to try to take my mind off things and cheer myself up. I retire during both runs after missing too many gates. I can hear people talking about me when I am at the post. 'What's she doing that for? That dog is weak as water. Used to be a good 'un, and all. What's she done to it?'

I walk off the field close to tears. I know the dogs are just reacting off me, they can sense my moods better than I can. I head for the car. I just want to go home and forget about it, forget everything for a while. But just as I'm about to start the engine there's a tap on the passenger-door window. Archie! Before I know it he's getting in beside me.

'Well, today's not your day, is it?'

I feel like crying again, but I won't in front of Archie. Instead I just sigh. 'You don't want to know.'

'It's not like you to be like this, hinny.'

I don't want to burden him with my problems, but somehow they all come pouring out.

204

Archie listens in silence. He doesn't speak for a while, and I'm sure he's thinking how pathetic I am. Then he says, 'You still happy at Fallowlees, though?'

'I don't want to be anywhere else, Archie, but I just can't see a way out of this mess. I don't want to start borrowing money, that'll just dig me deeper into the money hole I'm trying to haul myself out of. It all seems pretty hopeless at the minute.' I give a mad laugh.

'Well, I've got an idea that will go a long way to solving your problems.'

I turn to face him. 'Yeah?'

'Yep. You won't like it, mind.'

'Go on.'

'Well, you can sell Fly.' He looks at me, then turns away and gazes at something in the distance. 'Told you you wouldn't like it.'

'Sell Fly?' I repeat. Actually, though I don't admit it to Archie, it's not a totally original thought. It had crossed my mind one night as I lay there not sleeping, before I discarded it as unthinkable.

'I can't do that, Archie. I think the world of that dog. '

'Aye, I know. But think of it this way. You're running a business now and running a business requires some hard decisions. A fact of life, that. Think of her as an asset, and a valuable one at that. How old is she now?'

'Four,' I answer.

'That's what I thought. She's at the peak of her value right now. You can't gain any national points with her because of her eyes, she can't have pups, and you've got a pair of very capable work dogs in Roy and Alfie. Plus, you've got Len coming along grand. Let's face it, Fly sometimes gets pushed to

205

the wayside these days.'

'You're right, she's not getting as much work as she'd like.' I sigh. 'You should have seen her when I took her to Glanton, Archie. She was just so keen to run!'

We hadn't been intending to compete when I took Fly to the Glanton trials earlier in the month. It's a notoriously difficult trial due to its rebellious sheep—big, overbred, stubborn things—and we were only there for a day out and to look round the show. Yet when Fly saw the competition she wanted to run too—and ended up winning.

I smile as I tell Archie about that day. At the end of it I posed for a photo for the *Hexham Courant* with Fly and Roy, an arm round each dog. Fly had one ear up and one down, the way she does, and they both looked straight down the camera lens like a real family portrait. And now here we are talking about breaking up my happy family.

'I know what you're saying, Archie, but I just couldn't bear it.'

'Well, lass, it's just my opinion. Sometimes we can't see the solutions that are right under our noses.'

On the drive home I think about what he's said. It shocks me that I'm even considering it, and yet I know it makes sense. The fact is, it could save me from going under. Selling Fly could be my lifeline. As I turn into the lane that leads to Harwood village, I pull the car in at the side of the road and take out my mobile before I can change my mind.

'Archie, will you start putting out some feelers to see if anyone is interested in an excellent working bitch.'

Then I look into Fly's honest eyes and wonder what on earth I've started.

Whitehouse Farm on the edge of Morpeth was once a big poultry farm and one of the biggest egg producers in the region but its focus has now moved towards educating and entertaining the public. I am going to be part of the entertainment. It's a lovely summer day and the car park is packed. I go in search of Linda, who's in charge. I'm ridiculously early for my show. As usual, I couldn't sleep for worrying.

'We've put you down for displays at eleven and three. It's well advertised on the main board when people arrive, and it's on their maps, too. They won't miss it.'

I swallow hard.

Linda sees how worried I am. 'You'll be fine. I'll come down with you to introduce you before you start your show. You might want to go down there now and get unloaded, but if you're at a loose end the birds of prey display starts at ten. He just started last week but he's worth watching.'

I drive my car, laden with the adult ducks, down to the little enclosure. The sheep, ten yearlings, are there waiting for me and they run to the corner and watch me warily as I unload the ducks into the small pen that has been set up for them. The ducks quack indignantly as I shoo them in. Roy, inside the car, is watching. Some early visitors hang over the fence and one of them asks what time the show is.

'Great, we'll all be back then,' he replies when I tell him, and I feel anxious again. I put the dogs into one of the farm kennels then check my watch. I have nearly two hours to kill.

The birds of prey display is about to take place, and I wonder if I can pick up some tips in showmanship. However, I can't really relax, and come back, still miles early, to the field to look at the ewe lambs I will be demonstrating with. There are ten of them: half are Texels—fat, obstinate and awkward—and the other five are Mules. Up until this morning they've been in a large field of around twenty acres, free to roam where they please. Now they have less than an acre and are clearly unimpressed. The smaller field is for the benefit of the spectators; certainly not for the sheep.

I've been here for a couple of practices and the sheep worked well for Roy one day and Fly the next. They were used to dogs and didn't gallop about, which gave me confidence in my ability to show the dogs working in front of an audience. During rehearsals I had aimed the little flock towards tufts of grass and other landmarks in the field and had managed to keep them on target all the way. If I thought of it as just another trial, I told myself, it would be quite straightforward.

Now I'm not so sure. I look at the sheep and spot their flared nostrils and flicking ears and see 'trouble' written all over them. However, it is too late to do anything about that now. All I can do is sweat it out.

As eleven a.m. approaches a crowd begins to gather and I take Fly, Roy and Bill across to say hello. Roy is totally unfazed by all the attention and the children fawning over him. Fly, on the other hand, laps it up, giving one of her smiles as everyone makes a fuss of her. Bill is kept occupied by a young boy with a bouncy ball—Bill's always been a sucker for a toy.

Linda introduces me to the crowds with a big build-up. Everyone looks at me expectantly. My mind goes blank. 'Hello,' is all I manage, then I stumble and stutter as I try to remember my lines. I've never done any sort of public speaking before, never had any need to. It was so easy chatting away at the fence before, but now I am horribly self-conscious. Everyone stands there patiently, waiting. I blush and look around for help. I catch Linda's eye and she gives me an encouraging smile. I look at my feet, and there is Fly gazing up at me expectantly with her honest eyes. I start to tell my audience all about Fly—about her character, about her near-death experience, about her fight for survival and her recovery. I tell them about her amazing attributes, her loyalty, her devotion. The people are hushed—they're expecting great things of this dog now. I scan the crowd as I talk. There's a real mixed bunch here, from smart well-to-do types to much more casual sorts, who you wouldn't expect to see at an event like this, but they all seem to be interested.

I turn to Fly.

'Come bye,' I tell my dog, and she begins a fast outrun to the left. She is about halfway up the field when the sheep spot her and make a bolt for it. They gallop alongside the fence and the two at the front jump straight over it into the next field. They clear it with ease. I can hear excited noises in the crowd as they realise this is not what was supposed to happen. Fly, however, is unfazed, and carries on with the remaining sheep, gathers them up and sets them moving down the field at a steady trot towards me, for the crowd to get a closer look. A few more whistles to Fly and they trot off towards the first obstacle. Fly is listening well and the little group of sheep trots quietly through the hurdles I have built for them.

The night before, I decided to finish this part of the display in a traditional manner, putting the sheep into a little pen near the crowd. The previous night Roy and I had put them in without any problem, but I hadn't considered the effect the crowd would have on the already touchy creatures. As Fly draws the sheep close to the open pen, it quickly becomes apparent that things are not going to go smoothly. With a nifty turn, the whole bunch makes a dash for it round the pen and back up towards the far end of the field. Fly quickly retrieves them and we try again. I'm starting to feel nervous again. Fancy getting all these people to come and see me and I can't even manage a simple task like this! Just as I'm about to admit defeat, Fly edges the defiant sheep into the pen and I slam the gate shut. I flash a victorious grin at the audience.

'And that's exactly what we do at a sheepdog trial,' I say. 'The field may be a lot larger, but—' The crowd are staring at the pen behind me and I turn round just in time to see the last sheep clatter her way out over the back of it. I turn to the audience with a grin.

'Oops!' is all I can say. They laugh along with me and the athletic sheep get a resounding round of applause, far exceeding anything I could have expected had things gone to plan. Keen to redeem myself, I swap Fly for Roy (Bill is still playing football with the little boy behind the audience). I tell them that Roy is the best dog I have ever owned as far as talent goes, and then I set him to work with the little pen of ducks. I have been practising for some time at home with my Runner ducks, and while Fly and Alfie will also work them (Bill refuses to waste his time on something so ridiculous), their finesse is nothing compared to the quick responses and smooth movement of Roy.

I open the pen and watch the ducks waddle out. The crowd start oohing and aahing, pointing and laughing. I don't blame them—they make a fine sight, waddling in their upright manner, like feathered wine bottles with heads. I cast Roy around them and steer them through the miniature hurdles I have made for the purpose. They negotiate them deftly—these ducks are the athletes of the poultry world, and get their name from the fact that they run rather than waddle like other ducks. The little characters enthral the crowd. The ducks move as if Roy has them balanced on the end of his nose. I steer them back into the little pen and shut the gate.

'Now, you lot, stay in there,' I tell them to the crowd's amusement. Then I thank the crowd very much for their attention and breathe a sigh of relief.

Later on in the canteen I find myself sitting with Tom, the owner of the birds of prey, Steve the handyman, and a couple of girls who work in the petting zoo. Tom asks me how it all went.

'Well, not exactly brilliantly, my display is nothing to yours, you know.'

'Don't be daft, your dogs look amazing.'

I shrug modestly. 'They're great, I know, but I can't help but think I need to, you know, entertain more. It all feels a bit educational at the minute.'

'Once I saw someone at a show who made his ducks go through a little tunnel,' Tom suggests.

'Really? Maybe I should get hold of one. That would add a little bit of fun.'

'I could build you a seesaw if you think you could get them to go on it,' says Steve.

'Yeah,' says one of the girls. 'What about a slide or something?'

'Or a swing?' suggests the other.

'What you're missing is a bit of audience participation,' says Tom. 'Couldn't you get the kids involved the way I do?'

'I don't know about that. I don't think my dogs would work for anyone else. And I don't want to let them loose chasing the ducks. That would be utter carnage!'

'You could just bring some of the audience into the ring, then. They could be the hurdles.'

'You know, that's a really good idea,' I say, brightening.

When I leave for the day I'm full of ideas and renewed enthusiasm.

*   *   *

That evening I trawl the Internet. I manage to find an agility tunnel which is divided into a rigid half and a cloth half. As I press the 'buy' button I wonder whether the ducks will be able to push their way through it. I also buy some plastic hula-hoops. Getting children involved seems to be the key to livening up my show, and I decide to create a sort of slalom with the kids standing in the hoops as obstacles. Steve has agreed to build me a seesaw, though I don't know yet if such a thing will work. I also look on the Internet for a plastic slide. I haven't a clue how I'll get the ducks to the top, but when I find a cheap second-hand one that's bright pink— which seems to suit the quirkiness of the show—I buy that too.

When I've finished making my purchases I decide to unwind by taking Len out to do some training. He has been improving week on week and training him has been such a joy. He takes everything in first time and is always willing to please, in a manner that reminds me of Fly, but he also possesses the same style as his brother Roy. I know I shouldn't get carried away, but I am hopeful that he will make a trial dog and be ready for the nurseries in November. I let him loose in the front field and he casts out in a beautiful line and brings the sheep to me at a steady pace down the field. Michael's Mules are looking well—plump from the meadow grass. The five Suffolks are to the fore. They've realised they're better off with what's growing here than in the forest, but they can still be pests when they feel like it and often refuse to conform.

Even as the sheep come close to my feet one of them turns towards Len and decides to test his patience. She stamps her foot at him and refuses to go any further. I encourage Len to walk up and turn the sheep back to the others, but the bolshy thing makes as if she's going to chase him away. Len meets her head-on and gives her a sharp nip on her nose. Satisfied now that he is the boss, the Suffolk carries on back towards the group as if nothing has happened. It is often the case in work situations that a ewe will try to test a dog's strength, but it's the first time Len has come up against it and I'm pleased that he handled it with style and confidence as well as patience.

For the past few days I have been teaching Len a manoeuvre called the 'look back'. I split the group and Len moves one half of them to one side of the field. I then call him back to the other half, work him round the little flock and he herds them to the opposite corner of the field. After a while, when I think he has almost forgotten the first group, I tell

213

him to lie down and then I ask him to look back. He turns instantly and spots them; a quick whistle to the left and he runs off to gather the faraway group. The lesson is over when the two groups are reunited.

'That'll do, Len,' I call. And he rushes across for a fuss.

*   *   *

Sally, the peregrine falcon, is perhaps the most impressive of all of Tom's birds of prey. She looks superior to the other birds, like a beautiful, aloof ice-maiden. I have long wanted to see a peregrine in action and this afternoon will be my chance. Tom's got it all down to a fine art: a perfect balance of showmanship, breathtaking wonder and audience participation.

Tom has clearly had fun naming his birds. A huge and very impressive European long-eared owl is called Florence; a creamy white barn owl is Potter; two tiny kestrels are named Itchy and Scratchy after the cat and mouse characters from *The Simpsons*. Tom is a natural in front of an audience, and I envy his skill and the ease with which he banters with the crowd. I will never have his easy confidence. He puts on his gauntlet and collects some dead chicks. He begins the display with Potter the barn owl, telling the crowd about these amazing birds which can hear a mouse moving beneath many feet of snow. When Tom whistles at Potter, he sweeps from his post thirty yards away and lands carefully on the glove where he tears at the dead chick.

Next on the cards is Florence. Tom tells us that she's still a baby and therefore rather clumsy. He asks some children to sit down on the grass and Florence jumps over them, flapping her enormous wings and wafting them with cool air as she goes. The children scream with mock terror as their parents gasp from the crowd.

He saves Sally for the finale. Tom throws her into the air and she soars high above us and soon disappears from view. Tom carries on talking, showing no sign of concern, but I think most of us are wondering if we'll ever see her again. He gives a whistle and throws a lure into the air.

'Let's hear it, everybody. Give her a shout. One, two, three—SALLY!' We all call her name and on demand Sally comes tearing through the air like a bullet. Tom swings the lure on the end of a long rope and as she comes close he pulls it away so that Sally is shooting towards us just inches above our heads. Some people duck, others scream. Again and again she swoops and dives, and finally, when Tom thinks she has had enough exercise, he lets her catch the lure. The reward is always a dead chick.

*   *   *

My display has changed tenfold since that first day, and I'm more confident about it too. I still get terribly nervous beforehand and sometimes my mind still goes blank, but I think I'm on to a winner as far as entertainment goes. Tom has given me some tips, and just watching him has helped enormously.

The ducks, too, have had an education. I still leave the young chocolate Runners at home, feeling that they are too young to stand the vigour of the performance, but the adults are well rehearsed. Roy has adapted beautifully to working them, and he

215

knows exactly what is required of him. There is only one way to find out if I can pull this off in front of the crowd, and that's to give it a go.

Like I had the first time, I start by using Fly to demonstrate how to work sheep. The sheep are better behaved this time and my clever dog earns herself a large round of applause as the sheep go into the pen and actually stay there. The real 'show' bit of the show starts with Roy. Out come the ducks from their pen. Roy leads them around a little course to warm things up, and then I direct the ducks on to the seesaw Steve has built. It is enormous and perfectly balanced, but it requires all of the ducks on the far end for it to tip. As the ducks waddle up it, the tension in the crowd builds. They reach the highest point, look as if they are about to think better of being stuck in the air, then all five stretch their necks towards earth and the seesaw drops to the ground. They happily jump off, unperturbed. Next is the tunnel. They waddle into the rigid part but as they come to the cloth they have to get down ('Watch them duck,' I say, to groans from the audience) and push their way along. All the crowd can see is five little bumps progressing through it. They laugh and clap as I count the ducks out. Roy, who always seems so puzzled when the ducks disappear, then shoots through the tunnel himself just to check he hasn't missed any, winning himself a big round of applause.

My favourite part is the pink slide. I have built a ramp up to it; it is rather steep, but Roy manages to steer the ducks up one at a time. They wait for a second at the top then slide down at some speed into the little plastic-duck-filled paddling pool at the bottom. I ask if there are any volunteers who would like to help me by turning themselves into obstacles.

I am overwhelmed by children clambering over the fence to stand in one of the six hula-hoops positioned in the field. When they are all in place I get Roy to slalom the ducks around, making sure that he takes them as close as possible to the kids without actually touching them, and they all scream with excitement. Back and forth they go, Roy focused on his task in the same way he focuses on everything he does. Finally, to keep with tradition, I finish by rounding them into the pen.

*

One evening I get the phone call I've been dreading. Bob is a shepherd from Scotland whose collie is getting too old for the job and whose youngster isn't up to scratch. He's heard about Fly and wants to know more. I find it hard to summon up any enthusiasm as I talk to him, not least because Fly is right beside me in the kitchen at the time. Yet, somehow, I answer his questions. Then I quiz him on where he lives and his job, on his experience with collies—perhaps this is a bit patronising to him but he's undeterred, and a few days later he arrives at Fallowlees in his pickup.

I've left Fly running around outside. I know full well that if she dislikes someone she's not averse to giving them a sharp bite on the ankle when they're not looking. I wait to hear the barking. Perhaps she'll scare him away and I'll have an excuse to change my mind. I can't hear anything until I jump at a knocking on the door. When I open it, Fly is standing next to the tall slim shepherd.

I can't help it, but I like Bob instantly, and it's obvious that Fly feels the same. He tells me he's been a shepherd all his life and we seem to have a lot in common. I make tea and we sit down to a good old natter. I almost forget why he's here. Oh why does he have to be so nice? All the time we're talking Fly is lying by his feet under the table.

'Well, I reckon we should have a look at what this dog can do,' he says suddenly.

My heart does a somersault. I manage a nod, and somehow lead the way to the front field. I might still be chatting merrily but I feel bereft inside. The sheep are grouped in a tricky place in some rushes at the far end, but I've got no doubt in my mind that Fly can bring them in. With Bob watching us both, I give her a quiet 'Come bye'. She's off, and brings them to our feet without a further command.

I can tell that Bob's impressed. I don't brag about her other attributes—I don't want to or need to. Instead I tell him her weaknesses, with emphasis on the fact she has collie eye and can't breed.

'Could I have a go at running her?' he asks.

I give a small laugh. 'Of course, but don't expect her to listen. She's never worked for anyone but me.'

And it's true. My beloved dog won't take a step for anyone else, won't go for a walk if I'm not beside her. But there's no harm in trying. I show Bob my whistles and he follows right behind them on his own whistle. And Fly responds. I can't believe it. I've never seen her do anything for anyone else before but here she is following his commands. I stand there in a state of shock.

Bob doesn't need to see any more. He gives me a satisfied look.

'Aye, I think we'll get along just grand,' he says. 'I'll take her.'

'S-sorry?'

'Aye, I'll take her. You were right—she's a grand dog.'

Suddenly things start moving fast. I'm not really prepared for this. The pleasantness of the past hour has turned suddenly sour and my throat has gone tight.

Bob hands me an envelope and inside it is fifteen hundred pounds in fifty-pound notes. He doesn't even quibble about the sum. Fifteen hundred pounds. Enough money to pay Fly's vet's bill. The envelope feels thin for such a momentous transaction. Do I really want it? I want to scream, 'No! Take it away! She's not for sale!' but I just have to thank him and put the envelope in my pocket.

Bob asks me to put Fly in his pickup and she jumps into the front seat with little encouragement, just like she's done a million times for me in my car. Bob shakes my hand heartily. I can tell he's delighted with his purchase, and I know he'll be a good master, but my heart is breaking.

'Well, Emma Gray. It was a pleasure to meet you. If we don't meet again, good luck with your farm and your life,' he says, before moving to the driver's side and getting in.

I steal a last look at Fly. She looks so beautiful and intelligent, one ear up, one ear down, those dark wise eyes looking back at me, reading me. She will know that I'm upset, she can always tell. I want to explain everything to her, but I know that I can't. There is nothing to explain. I have no justification for what I'm doing. I am sacrificing my love for her for the farm and for my future.

Fly's own future will follow a different course from mine now. The dog who has given me and taught me so much drives away to a life without me. I watch the truck disappear away into the forest.

Chapter Twelve

Sometimes I think Fallowlees is a blessing and a curse. It has brought many things I am grateful for, but it has also brought hardship the likes of which I have never known before. I love it for the opportunity it has given me to stand on my own two feet, to be my own boss, and for providing me with a beautiful place to live. But it has forced me to make some painful choices, left me feeling isolated and lonely, and now it has forced me to make the hardest decision of all. I have sold my favourite dog in order to pay for her lifesaving operation.

At times the farm feels to me like a living, breathing thing, something that needs endless care and attention—like a child. And like a child, sometimes it is grateful for the attention I lavish on it and at other times it is mean and selfish and makes me wonder why I bother. Yet we have a bond, my farm and I—a bond that has been established since the day I moved in. In fact, I think, since the first time I ever saw it.

*   *   *

I have enjoyed my spell doing displays at Whitehouse Farm. I get better at the shows, and though I still get nervous beforehand I quickly find that I'm having fun. And I get to work my dogs every day. I like the social side, too, meeting the public and getting to know some of the fellow workers. But it's not earning enough to sustain me. The hour's drive there and back each day costs me too much, and I can feel that the dogs are getting a little bored too.

Tom echoes my feelings as we have lunch in the canteen. 'Yeah, it happens. Animals need a change in their routines, too. Yesterday Sally took off during a display and didn't come back till this morning. And during this morning's show she took off and killed a seagull.'

'Wow! That's amazing!'

'Well, yeah, it was pretty amazing but there were little kids watching and I think some of them got upset.'

'I'm starting to realise how true that old saying is: never work with children or animals. And there we are doing both!'

Actually, even the ducks are getting bored. They know the obstacles so well that it doesn't look as much of a challenge as it used to.

'Yesterday Bib didn't go up the seesaw,' I tell Tom. 'Instead he ran round underneath it and waited for the other four to land.'

'The little blighter!'

'Yeah, they nearly came down on his head. Everyone was holding their breath to see if he was OK. Luckily he was, but I think they're getting wise to the whole thing. And another time I was just putting them into the tunnel when Roy ran in and shot out the other side before the ducks even got in the entrance. I think he wanted all the applause for himself.'

Tom chuckles. 'Mind, that's nothing. You know my African pied crow, Chewy?'

'The one who looks like a magpie?'

'That's the one. Well, he's taken to landing on people's heads, which is bad enough, but the other day he had a massive dump on some poor woman at the same time.'

I howl with laughter.

'I know it's funny, but it's not good. I'll have to stop using him for displays if he carries on with it. And Potter isn't flying as well as he used to. We've got to think of the public all the time. It's what we're here for.'

'A guy came up to me this morning and told me his Staffy could herd ducks better than Roy, the cheeky sod!'

Our audience is such a mix, it's been quite an eye-opener for me. I tell Tom how someone watching me the other day had looked like such a hard nut. He had a shaved head and facial tattoos and piercings everywhere and the little lad with him, who was only about eight, had a Mohican. I made all sorts of assumptions about their characters, but when I got talking to him he told me that he'd brought his son specially to see all the animals, and he was passionate about them himself. He had dogs at home and he loved them to bits, and he was so enthusiastic about my collies. Apparently he'd had a collie when he was a little lad.

'I was just really surprised. He went against all my preconceptions.'

Tom nods. 'Mind, there's some right numpties as well. The ones that are always trying to touch the birds, even though the sign says, "Do not touch the birds." One of these days someone will get bitten and that will be the end of it all.'

'Yes, I had a crazy family like that yesterday. Did you see them? They tried to whistle at Roy while he was working the ducks and then tried to catch Simples and Alexander from the meerkat enclosure.'

'Yep, I couldn't forget them. They stole a load of stuff from the gift shop on the way out!'

I ask Tom what he's going to do when the school term starts again in September and he tells me he's going to stay on and do special experience days with the birds so that he can keep them fit over the winter. Ultimately, he hopes to save up for a golden eagle.

He asks the same of me. 'You could stay on here too, you know, if you had a word with Linda.'

I shake my head. 'The dogs and the ducks have had enough of two displays a day. I need to concentrate on my farm.'

'But can you make money out of it? I thought you said it wasn't that big.'

I've been thinking about this for a while now, and I decide to share my thoughts with Tom. I haven't told anyone else my plans apart from Archie.

'I've decided to try to make a living at what I'm good at. I mean, this has been fun, but I don't think my future is really as an entertainer. I'm going to concentrate on training dogs.'

'How would that work?'

'Well, since I've had the farm I've been approached by a few people asking if I could take their dogs and train them to work sheep. I've been doing it for myself for such a long time now, it feels like what I've been born to do.'

I tell Tom the story of my first dog, Bess, and all the hours we spent together. 'I reckon that's the way forward for me. That way I can concentrate on the farm a bit more, and I can do a bit of sheep work on the side for local farmers as well. And I know I'll always be in demand at lambing time, so that's one bit of guaranteed income at least.'

Tom looks impressed. 'Hey, Emma, sounds like

you've got it sorted then.'

*   *   *

I've been looking forward to the Kelso tup sale ever since Nikki and I put it in our diaries a few weeks ago, and now I need something to cheer me up more than ever. Even the dogs seem sad, reacting off my grief even if they don't actually seem to be missing Fly that much.

I've arranged to meet Nikki at Otterburn, where I leave my car and jump into her rather snazzier one: comfy seats, air conditioning, electric windows, a swish CD system. And not a dog hair in sight. I'm like a little kid fiddling with all the knobs and buttons.

'You need to get out more,' says Nikki, raising her eyebrows. We join up with the A68, which follows the Redesdale Valley towards Carter Bar, where England turns into Scotland. Looking at this bleak but beautiful part of Northumberland, the site of conflicts between England and Scotland since Roman times, helps to put my own worries into perspective. I lean back and enjoy the ride. We are climbing as we go, and my ears pop in protest.

'How's things, anyway? What about those hunky shearers?'

'They're great guys, but it wasn't like that.'

'Oh, Emma. Most girls I know would give anything to be around men as much as you are.'

'What—have their arm up a sheep's you-know-what? Covered in grease and itching all over after picking up fleeces all day till your back feels like it's breaking? Not to mention the five in the morning starts.'

224

'Yeah, well, you could at least flutter your eyelashes as you admire their skill with the clippers.'

'Those men are on the road all the time. Not much good for me. And if I stood there going all doe-eyed on them they'd tell me to get my lazy arse back to work! And you know well enough that most of the farmers I meet are twice my age. No, I think Fallowlees is turning out to be the big love of my life.'

Nikki snorts and follows with an anguished yelp. 'Ow! Have I told you yet how I got these bruised ribs?'

'No, you said you would today. What happened?'

'You know how I spend so much time on the road. Well, I was caught a bit short after too many cups of tea one lunchtime and I just couldn't find anywhere to stop. In the end I had to pull in to a quiet lay-by and hope no one went by. There I was, squatting down on the other side of the car, when the bloody thing starts to roll backwards down the incline. 'Course I pulled my knickers up mighty fast and legged it after the car.'

I'm already killing myself laughing.

'Glad *you* think it's funny. Anyway, I managed to get the door open but it was rolling too fast for me to get in and next thing I know the damn thing has swung out and clobbered me. I'm lying there in agony watching the company car carry on without me and land in a ditch at the bottom of the hill.' Nikki puts a comforting hand on her ribcage. 'They're starting to heal, but if I don't laugh much today, that's the reason. Bloody hurts when I do.'

'Oh, Nikki!' Tears are rolling down my cheeks. 'It could only happen to you.'

'Yep, you're not the first one to say that.'

Kelso hosts one of the biggest sales of male sheep in the country; everyone who is anyone goes to Kelso, and there are over six thousand rams to choose from. Three million pounds will change hands today as every breed imaginable goes under the hammer.

I can smell the tups as soon as we get out of the car—a distinct, musky aroma. They are at their physical and sexual peak, and every single one of them is giving off strong pheromones. This strong smell mingles with that of the dip some of them have been dressed with: bright orange for the Cheviots and some of the Texels, dark brown for the Suffolks, with an assortment of other colours on display. Each vendor keeps his sheep in his own pen in one of about twenty long marquees; some have brought more than eighty to market, though most have around fifteen to forty. Each marquee has its own auction ring so there are sales going on all the time.

The sellers are keen for their animals to look their best for this big day, and the tups have been well fed and nurtured. They need to be in top physical condition, anyway, in order to survive a season in which each one will be expected to service fifty ewes. Brimming with aggression, they look as if they are raring to go right now. They are fine-looking specimens—and don't they know it. Around them are piles of cabbages, a favourite food of the tups and a nourishing and cheap one at that.

The selling has already started when we arrive and we slip straight into the Texel tent where the auctioneer is in full swing at the ringside. As he belts out the prices at breakneck speed, I wonder if a newcomer could make sense of it all. It must sound like another language. But the men here are seasoned buyers and have no such problem. A nod here, a wink there, is all it takes to boost the bidding upwards. The Texel on sale now is a proud creature who runs round the ring showing himself off. When he bleats, issuing a deep and throaty call designed to attract a mate, it reminds me of the purring sound a ewe makes to a newborn lamb, though it's much louder and more aggressive. The hammer comes down. Sold for six hundred pounds. This fellow is on his way to a new life as lord of his very own harem.

As we're here purely for pleasure, Nikki and I move through each of the tents at our leisure, admiring the rams. There are so many breeds, from the squat little Beltex to the heavy Dorsets and the elegant Leicesters. I'm revelling in the hustle and bustle, and just being amongst all these like-minded sorts. I needed this break, I think. Our progress is slow as I keep bumping into people I know.

Conversation in these tents is limited to the condition of the tups, the weather, the price of lambs, the rising price of cull ewes. It would bore the pants off anyone else. Acquaintances I haven't seen for a while ask me how I'm getting on with my farm and I just smile and tell them everything is fine.

Trade is good and that makes for a happy atmosphere. The buyers are pleased with their purchases and the sellers are happy to have money in their pockets. Nikki and I pass the day chatting, and enjoying all the little dramas evolving around us as each sheep takes its turn in the ring.

As the day draws to a close, all the top-price tups are photographed for the papers. The most expensive has sold for ten thousand pounds, and several others have made prices in the mid thousands. They head home with their new owners in quad trailers attached to the back of wagons, ready to provide next year's crop of lambs.

As the crowds and the flock dwindle, Nikki and I make our way to the beer tent. It's a lively, noisy place; everyone is in good humour and feeling generous with their cash. The men all look smart in shirts and ties, flat caps and tweeds.

Later, when most people have gone home, the small crowd of us that remains heads to the Cross Keys pub in Kelso's cobbled town square. I am starting to feel the effects of the vodkas I have had, but I'm not ready for the day to end just yet. Nikki seems happy to tag along, even though she's not drinking.

As I'm talking to the auctioneers from my local mart in Hexham, I turn round and happen to catch the eye of a young man in another group standing beside a man in his forties who has a shock of blond hair. He smiles at me and I smile back before turning round to face my crowd again. He looks familiar and I wonder where I've seen him before. I decide it's from a Young Farmers' dog trial the previous year.

Gradually, our two little social groups merge, whether by accident or design I don't know. I learn that the blond man is called Alan McClymont and he has done well with his blue-faced Leicesters today. He is from a farm in the Yarrow valley, not too far from my parents' place. The younger man, who is tall and good looking, is called Daniel Walton, and used to be Alan's shepherd but he's now working on his family farm near Alston in Cumbria. I keep sneaking glances at him and he seems to be looking at me whenever I do.

When the time comes to leave, we find ourselves heading in the same direction. Dan spots a pickup piled with a load of cabbages, grabs one and throws it in the air. He looks across at Alan who has already run across the square. In the blink of an eye, a game of cabbage rugby has begun. The rules are a bit suspect and nobody scores any tries but it's fun while it lasts. The game comes to an abrupt close when I miss a throw from Dan and the cabbage meets a messy end on the cobbles. We laugh all the way back to the cars.

'Good to meet you both,' says Dan as we part company. 'See you around.'

Nikki's car flashes through the countryside.

'Dan was nice,' she says, glancing at me briefly.

'Yep,' I say. 'He was.'

*   *   *

A few days later a knock on my door terrifies the life out of me. I don't receive many casual visitors. The man standing there tells me he's from ITV. I must look dubious because he shows me some ID. They're filming a new detective drama in the north-east, he says, and he's spotted my place on Google Earth and wonders if he could look round and take some photos. I wonder if he's pulling my leg but he seems genuine. I invite him in and after a quick chat he goes upstairs while I put the kettle on.

As I busy myself in the kitchen, I can hear his footsteps, stopping and starting. Suddenly it freaks me out. What am I doing letting a stranger into my home? I wonder if I should make a run for it. I listen at the bottom of the stairs. I can hear the clicking of his camera. Well, he *seemed* pretty genuine, and why else would he want to take photos? It would be a bit of an elaborate ploy if he wanted to take advantage of me.

He comes back the next day with two others and they look round Redpath, too, which is where they eventually decide they'd like to film.

'It'll need a lot of work if you're filming inside,' I laugh. 'It's just an empty shell.'

But he tells me that will make their job easier, and it's amazing what the cameras can do.

The best thing about it all is that they will pay me. I book the pickup straight into the garage as soon as they've gone, trying not to dwell on the fact that if this had only happened sooner, I wouldn't have needed to sell my beloved dog. I hope I did the right thing. Are you happy with your new master, I wonder. Have you forgotten me yet, or do you sometimes wake up from your sleep, sniff the air and wonder why you are not in your kennel at Fallowlees?

*   *   *

The Wallington Estate, to which Fallowlees belongs, has been designated a 'low carbon village' by the National Trust, in a project supported by a big energy company. The plan has always been for the farm to make the most of renewable energy sources, and at long last it looks as if my windmill is finally going to happen.

I get a call from the Newcastle *Journal* wanting to come and talk to me about it. I suppose it makes a good story: big electricity company gives free windmill to poor girl in the woods. I'm happy to oblige—I'm fed up with the noisy, unpredictable old generator, of standing in the freezing cold and pitch dark in my pyjamas and wellies trying to fix it when it conks out. And if we happen to get a winter as bad as the last one, well, it seems unlikely, but I need to be prepared.

Jessica, the reporter, arrives in Harwood village in a snazzy two-seater, takes a look at the forest track and panics. She gives me a ring, wondering if I can pick her up.

'This road!' she exclaims as we bounce across the potholes together half an hour later. 'You must get fed up with doing this every time you want to go anywhere.'

'I suppose I just accept it as the price I pay for living in such a fantastic place,' I reply. 'Talking of which, do I get paid for this?'

She shakes her head. 'Sorry, we don't pay for interviews. But I could probably get you a free advert in the paper if you needed one.'

I show her around the farm and then we settle down with cups of tea in the kitchen for a chat. She seems fascinated in hearing about my life and how I ended up living in such a remote spot—I suppose it must seem a million miles from her own story. I thought the interview was going to be about the windmill but it's nice to talk about myself to someone who's so interested and I happily chat away for a couple of hours. She tells me excitedly that if all goes well, it should appear in Saturday's paper.

When Saturday comes I rush off to the nearest newsagents, half an hour's drive away in Rothbury. There's a pile of *Journals* in a stand right by the door and everyone's buying it today. I pick one up then stop dead when I see the cover. I can feel a flush building on my cheeks and spreading down my neck. There I am for everyone to see—it's quite a nice picture, actually—and underneath are the words, 'Wanted: man. Must have good sense of humour, a

4×4 and like sheep.'

I can feel myself cringing. When Jessica told me I could have a free advert, I wasn't expecting a lonely hearts ad! This must be the most public one ever!

*   *   *

Alwinton Show is the last show in the Border shepherds' diary, and is held on the first weekend in October in the gorgeous Coquet valley, with its springs and rainwater from the windswept Cheviot hills, winding its easterly way to the North Sea.

Alwinton is normally a sleepy village, but today the field behind the pub has been transformed by tents, marquees and trade stands as farmers and shepherds bring the best examples of their sheep to show and be judged. Even though the outbreak of foot and mouth led to a gradual dwindling in the entries to agricultural shows, Alwinton has always achieved good entries for the sheep classes, and this year is no exception.

The show is already packed and queues are forming along the road as young farmers direct the traffic and park the cars. People come from all over, from nearby towns and villages and even from as far away as Newcastle. The weather is overcast, and the field is already muddy, but it is October and to be expected.

The dog trial field, just next to the show field, usually generates a lot of interest, and as I'm first to arrive I'm also first to run. Alfie has a decent run, but without the benefit of watching the sheep's behaviour on the course, I miss a set of gates and even Alfie isn't quick enough to turn them on the right line in time. I decide to run with Roy in the afternoon and to have a look round the show beforehand.

I spend most of the morning mooching around the field taking in the trade stands. I watch the Cumberland wrestling, an unusual sport where two men (or occasionally women) grapple with each other, the winner being the person who puts the other to the ground. I watch the terriers racing each other to try to catch a fox's tail. I meander through the industrial tent where tables are laden with wonderful things to eat and drink, from scones to quiches, homemade cider to sloe gin. Flower displays sit proudly next to hand-carved shepherds' crooks and massive onions and leeks.

A farmer I know vaguely sidles up to me at one of the stands.

'Still single, eh?' He nudges me and gives a leery wink. 'It's a wonder, mind, after that plea of yours in the paper.' He puts his red, weather-beaten face up close to mine. 'It's coming up to winter, ya kna, nights are getting chilly. I'll keep ya warm if you like, snuggle in, eh?' He walks away, laughing at his own wit. I grit my teeth and smile sweetly. He's old enough to be my father, but I've had to get used to this sort of talk over the years. I know it won't be the only ribbing I'll get that day.

When I finally get to the sheep, I see people I know standing round the pens of beautifully titivated creatures, admiring and criticising. The breeds include Mules, Texels, Cheviots and Leicesters, but Blackfaces seem to dominate the field. The Leicester tup judging is under way and the judge is Alan McClymont, the man I met at Kelso. The breeders hold their animals while he performs a thorough inspection, examines their wool and even looks inside their mouths to see if their teeth are correct. Over by the ringside spectators, I recognise Dan standing with two young farmers, Nigel and Kevin, farmers' sons from near me. I compose myself, then make my way across to have a natter.

Dan looks pleased to see me, which gives me a buzz. He tells Nigel and Kevin about Kelso and the cabbage rugby game. We have a laugh, but we're also watching the judging carefully. We are all passionate about sheep and farming, which seems to be rare amongst the offspring of farmers these days. The rosettes and trophies are doled out and the sheep are returned to their pens, their owners either congratulating the judge or grumbling in the background that he doesn't know the back end of a sheep from the front.

I glance at my phone to see the time and realise I should be at the trial field getting ready to run, and to my surprise the boys decide to come and watch. Christ. I hope I can put up a good performance.

I stand at the post, aware of all three of them looking on expectantly. The sheep trot out to the post quietly enough, and I set Roy out on a right-hand outrun. He is about halfway up the field when one of the sheep starts to play up. The people at the top of the field manage to hold her with the group until he reaches them, but as soon as he's there she takes off again. Great, I think. Thanks for spoiling my chances. I bet I'm going to make a right idiot of myself now. But I was underestimating Roy. At the top of the field he fixes her with his eye and brings her to join the others. Next thing I know the little quartet are trotting at a nice pace in a straight line down the field with no signs of mutiny in their mottled faces. They pass me and carry on towards the gates, hit them perfectly, then carry on to the next set which has been the bugbear of the trial up until now. Few people have managed to hit them, but Roy and his obedient little packet trot through bang on. I can feel the nerves starting to build as I whistle to Roy to execute a tight turn at the gate. I'm on to a winner; the run has been smooth and straight, and all that's left is the work at hand, which Roy excels in: the pen and then the shed. In my head I have got the trophy in my hand and am filling it up in the beer tent, the boys looking on in admiration. I take the rope to the pen and open the gate. Roy is bringing the sheep at a nice gentle pace, I couldn't ask for more. But just as they are getting close, I see that darned Mule again, her head coming up as she realises the trap. Despite Roy's best efforts to stop her, she makes a dash for it, bolts right past Roy and jumps into the exhaust pen at the bottom of the field, which is where the sheep are supposed to go when the trial has finished. I turn to the judge, shrug my shoulders and shut the gate with a wry grin. That's sheepdog trialling for you, I think, as I take the three remaining sheep to join her. I can still clearly pick her out from the more docile animals already in the pen.

I go back to join the boys, who are having a good laugh at my expense.

'Hey, didn't you know you were supposed to get them all in that pen? Do you get bonus points for getting them to jump into the exhaust pen?'

I have to laugh. It's something I have learnt from working with sheep and from all the trials I've taken part in over the years. No matter what happens, don't take it to heart. And always be prepared to laugh at yourself.

We retire to the beer tent where we while away the rest of the afternoon with friends, discussing sheep and cattle shows and farming in general. Nikki is there with a crowd, too, and soon we are all in the Rose and Thistle having a dance and enjoying ourselves.

Nikki and I are staying with a friend in the village and just before we go Dan comes over and asks for my number.

'I'll ring you tomorrow,' he says.

Chapter Thirteen

Normally a farmer would choose to sell his stock at specialised sales throughout the year alongside other farmers selling similar stock. But sometimes, for whatever reason—a disagreement with a landlord, lack of children to follow in his footsteps, old age—he will sell the whole of his stock at a dedicated sale called a dispersal sale. Anything could go under the hammer: sheds, tractors, equipment, ewes, tups, the lot.

Today Don, an old farmer I've known for years, is selling up. He's great fun, a true salt of the earth character. He wears braces and smokes a pipe with which he wages an eternal battle to keep it lit. He has always been interested in breeding lines and his passion is Suffolk sheep.

The sale begins at midday, and I'm glad to see that many others have had the same idea as me and turned up to support him and to make sure that his stock doesn't go too cheaply. The good bloodlines and quality stock have brought people from all over the country and we crowd around the ring, which is set up a bit like a miniature stadium so that even the folk at the back can see the animals and get a good view.

The sheep are pedigree Suffolks, and they look fantastic. They have been coloured with a dark dip and groomed with a special brush to fluff up their coats. Their heads have been rubbed with baby oil to give them a glorious shine. They are trimmed and titivated to perfection and their rude health is abundantly clear. As they bound into the ring, one at a time, they seem to know that their duty is to look their best, and when they stand still they hold their heads proudly.

The catalogue gives the life story of each animal, whether it was a twin or single at birth, its pedigree and any other relevant facts. The ewe in the ring at the moment is the mother of twenty of the creatures that have just been sold. The blurb says she is a particular favourite of the farmer. Sure enough, Don is beside her, talking gently to her before getting down on one knee to stroke her head. She stands there, comfortable in the company of a man she has known all her life, oblivious to the crowd. The gavel falls and she is shooed out of the ring and the next animal runs in. Again and again they come, fantastic specimens of the breed. I am pleased to see that they are realising their full value and I look across at Don. His sorrow is tangible.

The last lot of the day is the stock tup, father of some of the previous lots and another favourite of Don's. He comes marching in, a powerhouse of masculinity. He may be a few years old but we have already seen the proof of his virility. It doesn't take long before the bidding has moved from the hundreds into the thousands. It carries on rising before the gavel finally falls at over three thousand pounds. The man next to me shuffles away towards the door, muttering to anyone who will listen, '*Pfff*, good price for an old tup, I'd say.'

He may be right, I think, but can you put a price on a lifetime's dedication?

*   *   *

I'm thinking about Don when I hear that the *Daily*

Mail want to interview me. The *Journal* was one thing, but is my life special enough to feature in a national newspaper? There must be women out there doing far more exciting things than I'm doing, and if it's farmers they're after, wouldn't it be more interesting to interview someone like Don, with a lifetime of stories to tell? They'd probably never get away from him, that would be the trouble! Once these old farmers start talking about their lives, the changes they've seen over the years, the trouble with the new generation, well, it's more than a newspaper article, that's for sure.

Vincent, the paper's reporter, rings from the pay phone in Harwood. They have decided the road is too bad for the photographer's car and wonder if there's any chance I could pick them up. I'm getting used to this. Luckily, now that the pickup is back in operation I can easily oblige.

There are three of them: Vincent, Alastair the photographer and Julie. She is a make-up artist—a make-up artist! Especially for me! It is all quite overwhelming, even before I meet them, and when they all greet me as if they have been waiting for the pleasure of my company all their lives, well, I am practically bowled over. I know it is part of their job to make the interviewee feel at ease. Whatever it is they teach these guys in journalism school, it works: I'm comfortable with them right from the start, and just wish I didn't feel so ashamed watching them load expensive camera equipment and smart make-up cases on to the sawdust in the back of my vehicle. The passenger area is little better with old sweet wrappers and the odd bit of sheep paraphernalia and—oh blimey!—there's even a large sheep syringe next to the handbrake which I hastily hide before

239

they notice and start wondering what it's for. I don't want them to get the wrong idea. I wonder if they're turning up their noses at that lingering doggy smell, but they all smile and chatter and act as if there's nowhere they'd rather be.

I take the long route back to the farmhouse and enjoy watching them marvel like excited children at how far away it is, the size of the fir trees and then that first glimpse of the farm. I show them round the grounds, feeling like a proud parent as they admire the view, and answering the usual questions about how I manage here on my own.

Alastair gets to work straight away. He asks me to put on some traditional working clothes—basically, a big jacket, jeans and boots—and to stand on the wall in front of the house as he snaps away.

'Put your foot up! Wonderful!'

'Look to the sky! Super!'

'Look like an empowered woman—hold that stick in a fist! Fabulous!'

Everything I do is showered with compliments and praise. This must be what it's like to be a model. Well, it makes a change from an audience of sheep and I am ashamed to say I lap up the limelight. Just this once, I decide to revel in the attention.

He shows me the pictures and they are surprisingly effective. I look like a real shepherd, hardened to the weather and the world; I think I even seem a little angry. We move into the field for some more shots, the sparse beauty of Greenleighton Moor behind us. Then I gather the sheep in with Roy's help so that they surround me and I meander through them. They are quite used to me now after all those hours training the dogs on them.

'Look stern! Smile! Don't smile! Look into the

distance! Look to the sun!' (Which makes my eyes water). The commands keep on coming.

'Go on, say it again,' says Alastair.

'What?'

'You know, that dog command.'

'What, you mean "away"?'

'Yes, that's the one.'

For some reason, all three of them find the tone in which I give this command completely hilarious

'Awaaaaay,' I say, and Roy is off again like a shot whilst my three new friends laugh and express their astonishment at what a clever dog he is. Vincent, in particular, is fascinated by him. He even tries to run him and has a go at copying my command.

'I don't sound a bit like that!' I say, wiping my eyes. 'No wonder poor Roy doesn't know what to do.'

'But I sounded just like you!'

Later in the kitchen it's Vincent's turn to get down to business. As he asks me about my background and my journey to this place, I find myself starting to relax even more and enjoy this little taste of celebrity.

'Do you feel closer to God here?' he asks out of the blue.

Uh oh, here we go, I think. Got to be careful here in case anything gets misinterpreted. I can see the headline now: 'Lone girl in the forest happily communing with God and nature.'

'No,' I say clearly. 'I do not feel any closer to God than anyone else.'

He asks if there is any romance in my life.

'No, not at the moment.' I've learnt my lesson after the *Journal*, no mention this time of disastrous dates or jokes about nice RAF lads rescuing me in the depths of winter if I get snowed in. And as I haven't heard a word from Dan since the Alwinton Show,

241

there's nothing to tell there; clearly another non-starter.

'I'm happily single,' I add firmly, hoping that I sound convincing.

'But one day?'

'Yes, of course, one day I'd like to share my dream with somebody, but for now I'm happy as I am.' Vincent nods his head seriously as if I've made the most profound statement. He fires more and more questions at me.

Alastair, who's been sitting quietly looking at all the outside shots he's taken, suddenly decides he wants something different.

'We need you looking a bit more feminine and girly. Could you put a dress on?'

'A dress?' I laugh. 'I don't think I have a dress.'

'Come on, you must have a dress lurking in your wardrobe somewhere!'

I rack my brains. Ah yes, there is something. 'I do have one, actually, but it's a ball gown.'

'Perfect,' says Alastair, so I traipse upstairs to put it on. The spare room doubles as my wardrobe since I haven't got round to buying any furniture yet, and my clothes are hanging there on the curtain rail. Right at one end is the dress. I haven't worn it for a few years now, but I remember the reaction I got when I did. It is electric blue, backless with a plunging halter neckline. It is ruched down the front and ends with a magnificent fishtail. It hugs every inch of my body like a close-fitting glove. As I put it on, I remember how much I used to enjoy dressing up. That sensuous feeling of silk sliding over my body. I pull it down and smooth it out. There, perfect. But what's that at the bottom? There is an unsightly stain, remarkably like puppy sick. Len, I bet. My moment of triumph marred by a dog! Typical!

I walk down the stairs, the silk trailing behind me. I feel a bit like a girl on prom night, or Cinderella all dressed up for the ball. They are waiting for me, these three strangers, and as I enter the kitchen they all stand there speechless for a moment. I suddenly feel a bit bashful.

Alastair speaks first. 'Darling, you look spectacular!' He asks Julie, who is also telling me how gorgeous I look, to do something with my hair.

'Could you put it up, do you think? Something incredibly glamorous. But sexy, too. And some make-up to match.'

He looks at me again. 'What about jewellery? Do you have anything suitably spectacular to go with this?'

I locate a cheap but very sparkly bright blue necklace and a large pair of dangly earrings. Even I can see that the result is great and I can hardly believe I'm going to be in one of the country's biggest selling newspapers looking like this.

I complete the look with a pair of black high heels and totter outside for another photo session. I stand on a rock and ask Roy to gather the sheep to me. I wonder if he'll think there's some impostor in my place but he's unfazed by my radical makeover and concentrates on the job.

Alastair must have taken hundreds of photos before he seems satisfied and calls it a day. And all the time I've been posing, Roy has been doing his job and keeping the sheep close by me. We finally retreat to the house to look at the results. Roy curls up on the seat in the kitchen, a little put out that he has been gathering sheep all day for no apparent reason. The pictures look amazing—that combination of sheep, moorland, and me in my dress, like Little Bo Peep in her best frock!

'What a picture!' says Alastair, pointing at one of them. 'I bet they use this one.'

Vincent nods. 'I'm going to write it up tomorrow and hopefully it will run on Saturday. Mind, you can never know for sure with newspapers, but that's the plan.'

'How many pictures will they use?' I ask.

'Well,' says Alastair, 'this one of you in the dress is a sure fire hit. And probably another one or two of you in everyday gear for contrast. I have to say, Emma, you look amazing.' I blush a little, but at the same time I'm very proud.

The interview is over and the photographs are done. I go upstairs and take off the beautiful dress, making a mental note to get the sick cleaned off. I give it a last stroke as I put it on its hanger back on the curtain rail, and wonder when I'll next get the chance to wear it.

Alastair and Julie are already loading their equipment into my pickup when I come back down. I notice that Julie has nearly as much stuff as Alastair. Vincent is sitting at the table making notes.

My mobile rings and it's an unknown number. I wonder if I should just leave it. I look at it for a couple of seconds, then, reluctantly, I answer.

'Hi, Emma, it's Dan . . . from Alwinton.'

As if I'd forget! I walk to the next room for some privacy.

'Hey, hi! How you doing?' *A phone call, not a text,* I'm thinking, *how delightfully old fashioned!*

'I'm good, thanks. Listen, I'm sorry, I would have been in touch sooner but I lost my phone . . .'

Really?

'No problem. You been up to much lately?'

'Just been gathering the hill today, but I got an early finish and wondered if you'd like to go out for something to eat tonight.'

Don't seem too keen. Play it cool, tell him you're busy. In fact, why not tell him you're in the middle of a photoshoot.

'I'd love to.' *Yaaaaaay!*

'Great, where would you like to go?'

'Well, we could meet in a pub halfway if you like.' The one I suggest is far closer to me than to him. Forget equality—let's see what he makes of that.

'Nah, don't worry about that. I'll pick you up. We can make our minds up then.'

'Er, do you remember where I live?'

'Yeah, course I do, it will be fine. I'll give you a ring if I get lost. I'll be with you at about six. Is that OK?'

'Sure, fantastic! I mean, I'll see you then.'

Vincent looks up as I walk back into the kitchen. 'You look happy.'

'Yes, I met this guy at a show recently, did I tell you about it? He told me he was going to ring, but then . . .'

Crikey, why am I blurting all this out?

Vincent gives me a quiet smile. 'Good luck,' he says.

*   *   *

The article duly appears in the paper. It's a big story, and they use lots of pictures, but my first reaction is disappointment as they didn't use any of the pictures in the ball gown. I start reading it, trying not to care, and after a while I think that it was probably for the best. They were beautiful photos, but they were an illusion and didn't show me for the shepherdess I am. I hear later that the powers that be at the *Daily Mail* vetoed them as they thought they looked Photoshopped! But I'm delighted with the article Vincent has written. He does gush about me in a way that makes my cheeks burn, but I'm flattered, too—what girl wouldn't be, reading this about themselves? *'She has tumbling auburn curls which have been loosely pinned back to reveal the most striking blue eyes I've ever seen,'* he writes. *'It would take a much harder man than me to refuse this gorgeous specimen anything she wanted.'*

I have a good laugh to myself. Something tells me there's going to be more ribbing at the mart.

However, it's an affectionate piece and an accurate depiction of my life, and I can hardly mock Vincent when I come across like a giddy young girl myself at the end of it, skipping with delight after my phone call from Dan. But that hardly matters now: Dan and I have started seeing each other.

When Julie came back into the kitchen and heard that I had a date she had insisted on doing my make-up and my hair. 'You're a bit dramatic for a night out in the pub at the minute, if you don't mind me saying,' she said, looking at her earlier handiwork. 'Don't get me wrong, it'll look great in the pictures, but you need something a bit more subtle for now if you don't want to scare the poor chap off.'

She also took down my hair, brushed it and pinned it loosely back. 'There, this is something you can manage yourself every day.'

Dan turned up bang on time in a big silver pickup, so it was a good start, and we decided to head into Newcastle and have something to eat there.

The meal itself was a disaster. Dan had something

vaguely resembling a pizza with such a generous helping of raw onions it was virtually inedible. My cold duck salad was little better, the duck tasting like sawdust. But we hardly noticed the food. I don't think there was a second of silence the whole evening. We had so much in common, and so many stories to share with each other.

Of course most of the conversation revolved around farming—marts, dogs, sheep. Dan turned out to be a huge fan of Blackfaces and could while away hours talking about their attributes. When I protested about how unmanageable they are with their wild nature and unpredictability, he always had an answer. He'd defend those wily creatures to the hilt. I tried to win him over to my beloved Mules, but it was a losing battle since a Blackface is required to produce a Mule in the first place. In the end, we agreed to differ.

Dan told me about his little Border terrier bitch, Trixie, who had cost him his front tooth when he defended her against a gamekeeper intent on shooting her. And once we were on the subject of dogs, well, I could probably talk for ever.

Chapter Fourteen

It is January, I have been living at Fallowlees for almost a year and I am currently busy training a young dog called Max. I take him out to the pen, a big round pen with no corners for the sheep to huddle in. It keeps the sheep moving and is ideal for training young dogs. The sheep—five black and white Jacobs I have bought specially for the job— seem to roll their eyes when they see us coming and I don't blame them. Max is a menace. A farmer brought him to me saying he was a handful and it was not long before I learned he was not exaggerating. The moment Max sees the sheep he starts to scream with excitement, pulling me towards them. I clip a muzzle on him before we get any closer. I let him loose in the pen and rather than run around the sheep he launches a full-scale attack. The Jacobs are wise to the ways of dogs and rush to my feet for protection. Max, too, knows that he can't touch them when I am near. Instead, he flies round them until, ten minutes later, he's exhausted and I can get him to lie down. This dog is going to take some work, but at least he is keen.

I have started my new business. Frustrating at times but it's what I'm good at. After my stint at Whitehouse I was inundated with people ringing up asking me to train their dogs. I still do some freelance shepherding and I still work my own dogs wherever I go, but my dog-training dreams have turned into a reality.

When I think Max has had enough for now, I take out my own youngsters. Blue is a chestnut red bitch fathered by Alfie. She has her father's obedience and speed, but is more blessed in the brains department than my lovable goon, which can't be a bad thing. Boris is a son of Roy, nearly identical in looks to his father, small, dark and swarthy, disobedient to the last but with incredible natural ability. They are my pride and joy right now and I have high hopes for them both.

As I put my youngsters back into their kennel, I hear a shout. Archie has made the journey to Fallowlees in his little Suzuki. We stand for a while admiring the view. The snows of December and early January have abated leaving the ground looking tired and grey, but still beautiful.

'It's as pretty as a picture, isn't it,' he says, shielding his eyes from the low winter sun. 'Talking of which, what happened with your film people?'

'Oh, I hardly noticed they were there. I thought it was going to be really exciting, but it was just a load of big buses parked at Redpath and lots of people hanging about. I'm sure they were busy but they looked bored most of the time. If you go inside Redpath now, in one room they've wallpapered a wall—just one wall, mind. I guess it'll look as if the whole room is decorated when the programme goes out.'

'Clever business, eh. You should have got them to decorate your own place at the same time.'

'Yeah, that would have been good. Fallowlees is never going to be featured in *Homes and Gardens*, that's for sure. But I'd rather live here in a hovel than have a palace somewhere else.'

'I'm pleased to hear it. Now, is there any tea on offer?'

We leave the sharp winter chill for the warmth of

the kitchen. The Rayburn has been a godsend and hasn't let me down.

As the kettle boils, Archie asks how I managed during the snow. 'Bet you didn't expect this year to be as bad as last. None of us did.'

I tell him that we got snowed in a few times, that sometimes the snow was up to my waist, but Dan's pickup could make it out most of the time. 'He put tyres as big as a tractor's on it, so we were never cut off for long. And we made sure we had plenty of supplies, just in case. It never came to eating the dogs anyway.'

'Aye, it's good to see you've got someone to keep you warm at night now,' he says winking.

Dan and I started to see a lot of each other after that first date. And he even saw me in the electric blue dress when we went to the Northumberland County Ball together. I was so happy that night. It seemed a perfect way to be ending an epic year of change, lows and highs.

I laugh. 'Yes, Archie, your quest is over at last.' I pour the tea. 'Sorry I haven't got any goodies for you.'

'Ah, I was expecting as much.' He pulls out an old ice-cream carton and puts it on the table in front of us. Inside are some of Eileen's buttered scones.

'Oh, Archie,' I say as I bite into one. 'I've missed you so much.'

'Aye, well, things change, we all move on. Now, tell us what's fresh. I see Len is doing champion in the nurseries.'

I'm proud of Len. I tell Archie he's been running well and has picked up a prize in every trial we've entered so far, apart from one where he had a sly nibble on the way round. He's a plucky little character.

'And how's Dale running?' I ask him.

'Oh, grand, fit as ever. We get to Fairspring when we can. Got to keep Liam on his toes.' Liam's been working full time at Fairspring since I left, and I've heard that he's taken to it like a duck to water.

Archie pushes the carton towards me. 'Go on, have another. You don't need to worry about your figure now.'

'Hey, I seem to remember you telling me that men would like a bit of flesh.'

'I just like to see a lassie enjoying her food. There's too much faffing around with diets these days. Anyway, tell me about this place. You're obviously full of busy.'

'Do you know, it's never been better. Dan and I are building up our own little flock. I know you'll think I'm mental, but lambing is still my favourite time of year. Lambing our own sheep on Fallowlees is going to be magic. And I'm already booked in on another farm.'

Archie wags a finger at me. 'Now don't go overdoing it!'

I shake my head. 'It's different with two of us. When I'm away Dan can be here. We'll manage. Speak of the devil.'

I hear Dan's pickup pulling up outside and Dan strides in and greets my old friend. I ask Archie if he'd like to see our sheep, and all three of us traipse outside. Roy and Alfie are waiting in the porch where they both have baskets now. They come in at every opportunity, particularly when they have dirty paws.

I cast both of them round the front field to gather the ewes. The Mules trundle towards us, heavy with pregnancy.

'I see Emma won the battle of the breeds,' says

251

Archie.

'Not really,' I say smiling, 'the Blackfaces come next week.'

The sheep are healthy and contented, and we stand watching them for a while, the dogs keeping them in check with gentle movements. I look out across my kingdom and everything is perfect.

Afterword

I am a different person today from the twenty-three-year-old who packed up her bags and left her fiancé one autumn day. My fiery temper and impulsiveness have cooled down; I am much more measured in the way I do things. My calmer temperament has paid off in my dog training, too. Dogs like somebody who is constant and even, not inconsistent and moody.

This past year, my second at Fallowlees, has been a whirlwind from start to finish. Dan and I seem to pool every bit of cash we earn into buying more sheep, and are building up quite a flock. We now have Texels, Mules, Blackfaces, the Jacobs and of course my five Suffolks who have so far, apparently happily, stayed put.

In some ways things are much easier. The generator has been replaced by my windmill, which provides a nice clean energy supply and saves me a fortune as well. And having someone to share my worries with is a huge help. But a farmer's life will always be a tough one, and I'll be the first to admit that farming and I fall out from time to time.

I still find some of the jobs emotionally difficult. Caring for ewes and lambs all spring and summer only to send them to slaughter in the autumn and winter is a hard thing to do. I go to such trouble to ensure that my flock have the best life they can possibly have. If I see one with a broken leg, I set it with plaster of Paris and keep him or her isolated until it heals. If another is sick, I am not happy until I know what the problem is and I have cured it. It strikes me that it is like healing the wounds of a convicted man so that he can be healthy to swing in the gallows.

I can remember to this day putting down my first lamb. I remember the animal himself, and I remember crying for hours afterwards.

And yet I count myself the luckiest person in the world. There is nothing else I would rather do, and I still can't quite believe my good fortune.

*   *   *

In the summer Dan and I travelled down to Surrey with Roy to have another go in the English national trials. We had a cracking run with particularly difficult sheep to contend with and ended up in the top five, and qualifying for the international in Scotland the following month. Sadly, we didn't make the final cut, but it fed my desire to come back and win it one day.

Roy might be my star, but my other dogs are proving themselves too. Alfie won a local trial last week and hopefully he will join Roy at the national next year. He remains as dippy as ever but loyal to the last. Len has turned into a top-notch working dog as well as qualifying for the nursery championship, where, if he couldn't better Alfie's achievement the previous year, he gave a good account of himself.

Dear old Bill is still the same as ever, bursting footballs and digging for moles. It saddens me to realise that he is an old man now, deaf and with failing eyesight, but he seems happy bumbling about.

Bess, my very first dog, is still going strong at Muirfield where she even manages to drag herself off her chair on occasion to join the other collies gathering the sheep, though these days she chooses to do this from her viewpoint on the back of the quad bike.

As for Fly, I've heard that she is going well for Bob up in Scotland, but I know that it would be too upsetting for me to ever see her again. I had to make some tough choices during that first year at Fallowlees, but selling Fly is the only one I deeply regret. Sometimes I also wish I had kept my job at Fairspring, even though I don't see how I could have carried on there and taken on what I'm doing now. But I loved that job dearly, as well as all the people who went with it—Archie, Ken, Hilary, Michael and Liam.

*   *   *

A lot of people seem to think that what I'm doing is a big deal for a woman. I may have been the only single female applicant for Fallowlees, but the fact is, there are a lot of women running farms today or who have done so in the past—and they have done so quietly, with no recognition. Capable women from all walks of life are struggling to make ends meet while striving to keep their dreams alive. I don't think what I have done is anything special, it is just that I've been lucky to have been given the chance to tell my story by the Little, Brown Book Group.

I have wanted to be a farmer right from the days pottering about in the lambing shed as a little girl, and while my parents never thrust farming on me, they have always been supportive. But they have also encouraged me to be independent and to stand on my own two feet, and for that I am eternally grateful.

Most of all, I am grateful to my dogs. They are the very reason I am receiving the recognition and respect that is coming my way. Without my dogs I would be a different person. To them I owe it all.

Emma Gray, December 2011